EnglishSmart — Grammar Grade

Contents

1 Nouns and Noun Use

A **Compound Noun** is formed when two or more words are put together.
Examples: flashlight, fireplace

A **Collective Noun** represents a group of persons, places, or things.
Examples: audience, crowd, crew

Exercise A

In the space provided at the end of each sentence, state whether the underlined noun is simple, proper, compound, or collective.

Do you remember what simple or proper nouns are?

1. The <u>band</u> played a marching tune. _____

2. <u>Dr. Parker</u> visited his patients in the hospital. _____

3. The <u>sheep</u> grazed in the meadow. _____

4. The <u>child</u> enjoyed an ice cream cone. _____

5. The <u>firemen</u> were able to put out the burning blaze. _____

6. The bowl was filled with a <u>bunch</u> of grapes. _____

7. The <u>pack</u> of wolves lived together. _____

8. The new automobile had all the latest safety <u>features</u>. _____

9. Professor Atkinson worked at the <u>University of Toronto</u>. _____

10. He tied his <u>shoelace</u> tighter. _____

11. The boys finally won the <u>game</u>. _____

12. Please put the <u>pile</u> of paper into the drawer. _____

Let's now look more closely at compound nouns.

Compound Nouns can be formed in three ways:
1. joining two nouns together to form one word
2. placing two words next to each other without joining them
3. using a hyphen to link two or more words

Exercise B

Underline the compound nouns in the following sentences.

There are 16 compound nouns in the 10 sentences below.

1. My father's brother-in-law was a fireman.

2. In our classroom, we had a tomato plant on the window sill.

3. My parents pay fire insurance on our home.

4. In his bedroom he has a fireplace.

5. When you get into a car, be sure to put on your seat belt.

6. Always keep a flashlight in the trunk of the car.

7. When she is older, she is going to be a baby-sitter.

8. After grade eight, we will attend high school.

9. He wants to get a motorcycle when he is old enough to drive.

10. She is the great-grandchild of her mother's grandmother.

Collective Nouns represent groups of people or things.

Example: The crew is busy preparing for the launch of the new ocean liner.

The word "crew" is a collective noun referring to all the people working on the ocean liner.

Exercise C

Underline the collective noun in each group of nouns below.

Remember: A collective noun may look like a singular noun but it represents a group of things or people.

1. flock birds   2. army soldiers   3. sailors navy

4. person group   5. fan audience   6. witness jury

7. father mother family   8. singer orchestra   9. people crowd

10. player team   11. students class   12. member committee

Verb Agreement

When a collective noun is used as a subject of a sentence, it will have either a singular or plural verb depending on the meaning of the sentence.

Example (1): The crowd cheers the winner of the race.
In this case, the collective noun "crowd" is referred to as a single unit and requires the singular form of the verb "cheer" which is "cheers".

Example (2): The family like to read books together.
In this case, the collective noun "family" represents the individuals within the family and the verb must therefore be plural.

Exercise D

Select the correct verb to suit the meaning of the collective noun in each of the following sentences.

> Read each sentence carefully to see whether the meaning involves the individual members of the group or whether it refers to the group as a single unit.

1. The army _____ (protect, protects) the citizens of the country.

2. The army _____ (visit, visits) their family whenever they can.

3. The team _____ (play, plays) many games in a season.

4. The team _____ (chooses, choose) their own personal equipment.

5. The audience _____ (applaud, applauds) the performance.

6. The audience _____ (finds, find) their seats before the performance begins.

7. The family _____ (eats, eat) dinner together.

8. The family _____ (go, goes) home at different times after dinner.

Noun Plurals

To form the plurals of simple nouns, apply the following rules:

1. in many cases, just add "**s**".
2. if a noun ends in "**s**", "**x**", "**ch**", or "**sh**", add "**es**".
3. if a noun ends in "**o**", and there is a vowel before the "o", add "**s**".
4. if a noun ends in "**o**", and there is a consonant before the "o", add "**es**".
5. if a noun ends in "**y**", and a vowel comes before the "y", add "**s**".
6. if a noun ends in "**y**", and a consonant comes before the "y", change the "y" to "i" and add "**es**".
7. if the noun ends in "**f**" or "**fe**", change the "f" to "v", and add "**es**".

Exercise E

Refer to the rules and make plurals of the singular nouns below. Place the plural words and the rule numbers in the spaces provided.

Singular	Plural	Number
1. ship	_____	_____
2. knife	_____	_____
3. hero	_____	_____
4. country	_____	_____
5. cowboy	_____	_____
6. bush	_____	_____
7. zoo	_____	_____

Changing Verbs to Nouns

Nouns can be created from verbs.

Example: "**Play**" is a verb and "**player**" is a noun formed from the verb.

Exercise F

From each of the verbs below, create a suitable noun.

1. sing _____
2. run _____
3. dance _____
4. swim _____
5. hike _____
6. teach _____
7. bake _____
8. climb _____
9. drive _____
10. work _____

CHALLENGE

Can you create the noun for each of the following?

1. One who creates art is an _____ .

2. A person who types is a _____ .

3. A person who specializes in mathematics is a _____ .

4. A writer of books is also known as an _____ .

2 Pronouns

Types of Pronouns

A pronoun functions as a noun in a sentence. Often, a pronoun takes the place of a specific noun in a sentence or previous sentence in a paragraph. The noun that a pronoun replaces is called an "antecedent". A pronoun must agree in number and gender with its antecedent.

Example (1): The train was late because **it** had many stops to make.
The pronoun "it" refers to its antecedent noun "train".

Example (2): Susan left the book in the classroom as **she** didn't have time to read it.
The pronoun "she" agrees in gender (female) and number (singular) with "Susan".

Exercise A

In each of the following sentences, circle the proper pronoun.

1. The boys played baseball during recess; (he she they) finished the game just as the bell rang.

2. Paul and Richard were late for school because (he they it) missed the bus.

3. I will be forever grateful to my teacher who helped (me I my) improve my reading skills.

4. The students enjoy creating artwork after they finish (their our your) other work.

5. The bell will ring in the schoolyard but we may not hear (them it those).

6. In the summer, Eric and Josh will go to the cottage where (we they he) will have lots of fun.

Demonstrative Pronouns

These pronouns identify specific nouns.

Examples: **This** is my desk.   **Those** are his books.
That is my classroom.

Interrogative Pronouns

These pronouns ask a question.

Examples: **Where** is my lunch box?
Which of these hats is yours?

> Using a demonstrative pronoun is like pointing to something by using language.

Put suitable demonstrative or interrogative pronouns in the following sentences.

1. This is my coat, but _____ one is his?

2. _____ one of my friends should I invite to the Blue Jay game?

3. _____ is your school located?

4. You like that one but I would rather use _____ one.

5. _____ are the best skis. They are even better than these.

6. _____ will you arrive and _____ direction will you be coming from?

7. _____ will be attending the meeting and _____ will it be held?

8. _____ will we be in 20 years? _____ is a tricky question.

A **Relative Pronoun** relates a dependent clause (one that does not stand alone) to the rest of the sentence.

Example: This is the new car **which** my father bought today.

The relative pronoun "which" connects the dependent clause "which my father bought today" to the rest of the sentence.

Rules: 1. use "who" when relating to people
2. use "which" when referring to other living creatures and to things
3. use "that" for either persons or things

Exercise C

Refer to the rules above and place the proper relative pronoun in each of the following sentences.

1. Sara was wearing the new sweater _____ she received as a birthday gift.

2. The tree _____ was in the backyard was the tallest in the neighbourhood.

3. His uncle _____ was visiting from Vancouver stayed for two weeks.

4. He chose to volunteer for the charity _____ helped the homeless.

5. Jenny was the one _____ did not show up.

6. The car _____ is parked on the driveway belongs to Uncle Bob.

7. Don't touch the vase _____ Mrs. Kennedy put on the coffee table.

8. The boy _____ hit three homeruns is Keith.

A **Reflex Pronoun** refers to its subject.

Example: She helped **herself** to some cake.

Exercise D

Put the proper reflex pronoun in the space provided in each of the following sentences.

1. We asked _____ whether or not we should have made the trip.

2. He pushed _____ to the limit and won the race.

3. The Maple Leafs prepared _____ for the big game.

4. We surprised _____ when we were so successful on our English test.

5. My dog hurt _____ when it tried to jump over the fence.

Do not use a reflex pronoun in place of a subject or object in a sentence.

CHALLENGE

In 5 of the following sentences, there is a misused reflexive pronoun. Cross it out and replace it with a proper pronoun.

1. You may call John or myself for the information.   _____

2. Frank and myself are in charge of the group.   _____

3. Patricia wanted all replies to go to herself.   _____

4. Myself, I prefer chocolate cake.   _____

5. You yourself can make the right choice.   _____

6. Himself is looking for someone to assist him.   _____

7. The teacher gave Daniel and myself some books.   _____

Sometimes, a reflex pronoun is used with its antecedent for emphasis. Which of the above sentences provides an example of this use?

No. _____

Pronoun Cases

1. Subjective case: I, you, he, she, it, we, they, who, whoever
2. Objective case: me, you, him, her, it, us, them, whom, whomever
3. Possessive case: my, mine, your, yours, his, her, hers, its, our, ours, their, theirs, whose

The subjective case is used when the pronoun is the subject of a sentence.

Examples: **I** went for a walk. **We** went for a walk. **They** went for a walk. **You** went for a walk.

The objective case is used when the pronoun is a part of the predicate and specifically the object of the verb or of a preposition.

Examples: Julia thanked **him**. Julia thanked **them**. Julia thanked **us**.

Examples: Objects of prepositions (underlined):

John threw the ball <u>to</u> **her**. John smiled <u>at</u> **you**. John walked <u>around</u> **us**.

The possessive case is used to show ownership.

Examples: This is **my** car. That was **our** house. This is **your** hat. That dog is **mine**.

Exercise E

In each of the following sentences, fill in the blanks with the proper pronoun from the choices in parentheses.

1. _____ (whose, who, whoever) books were left on the floor?

2. I looked everywhere for _____ (mine, my, its) house key.

3. _____ (myself, I) will speak first.

4. _____ (whomever, whoever) wins the race will receive a prize.

5. The teacher asked Martin and _____ (I, me) to help arrange the desks.

6. The story interested _____ . (us, we)

7. To _____ (whom, who) are you asking the question?

8. Paul and _____ (I, me) will meet on Saturday.

9. The guest speaker answered questions from _____ (whomever, whoever) asked them.

10. It will be _____ or _____ (them, they / we, us) who will be chosen.

11. Have you lost your eraser? I think this is _____ (hers, yours).

3 Descriptive Words and Phrases

Adjectives and adverbs are descriptive words that add meaning to a sentence by giving the reader additional information.

An adjective describes a noun or a pronoun, often the subject or object of a sentence.

An adverb describes a verb, the action in the sentence. Adverbs often end in "ly" and answer the question "how".

Example: The **tall** boy walked **slowly** down the road.

"Tall" is an adjective describing the noun "boy"; "slowly" is an adverb describing the action of the verb "walked".

Exercise A

Underline the adjectives and place parentheses ( ) around the adverbs in each sentence below.

Remember: A subject is the doer of the action in the sentence. An object is the receiver of the action in the sentence.

There is at least one adjective and one adverb in each sentence.

1. The sly fox slipped quietly through the woods.

2. The black cloud hovered menacingly over the playing field.

3. John, the oldest boy in the class, spoke confidently.

4. The boys often enjoyed playing exciting computer games.

5. The red bicycle suddenly broke down in the middle of the trip.

6. They carefully entered the cold, dark cave.

CHALLENGE

Some words can serve as both adjectives and adverbs. For the sentences below, state whether the underlined words are acting as adjectives or adverbs.

1. The score was a <u>far</u> cry from what we expected. _____

2. He was in great shape and ran <u>far</u>. _____

3. She arrived <u>first</u> because she had a ride. _____

4. This is the <u>first</u> time we have been here. _____

Adverb and Adjective Phrases

A phrase is a group of words that usually begins with a preposition.
Phrases describe nouns, pronouns, and verbs in a sentence. Adverb phrases often answer the questions where, how, or when the action took place.

Example: The girls **in our class** played **on the swings**.

"In our class" explains who the girls are, and is, therefore, an adjective phrase. It is a phrase because it is a group of words beginning with a preposition (in).

"On the swings" explains where the girls were playing. It is a phrase because it, too, begins with a preposition (on).

 Exercise B

**Underline the adjective phrases and place parentheses ( )
around the adverb phrases in the sentences below.**

> Check to see whether the phrase answers the questions "when",
> "where", and "how". If so, it is likely an adverb phrase.

1. The walk to the store was very difficult during the storm.

2. In the morning, the animals in the barn were fed.

3. The leader of the pack was the large grey wolf.

4. The pens in the desk were the property of the boy in the third row.

5. At the game, we ate our lunch of sandwiches and cookies.

6. During his speech, he dropped the notes of the project.

CHALLENGE

**Some words are unnecessary because they are redundant. Cross out the
unnecessary adverb in each sentence.**

> "Redundant" means that a word or idea is repeated unnecessarily.

1. He was asked to repeat again his question.

2. They should all cooperate together.

3. The students were told to finish up their schoolwork.

4. They returned back from holiday.

5. They divided up the winnings.

A **Preposition** is a connecting word that connects a noun or pronoun to other parts of a sentence.

Prepositions are also used to introduce adjective and adverb phrases.

8 rules for frequently misused prepositions:

1. **at, with** – use "at" with a thing; use "with" when relating to a person.

2. **among, between** – use "among" when referring to more than two; use "between" for two.

3. **beside, besides** – use "beside" to mean next to; use "besides" to mean other than or as well as.

4. **in, into** – use "in" to mean within something or somewhere; use "into" to mean from outside to inside.

5. **differ from, differ in** – use "differ from" to show difference between two people; use "differ in" to state in what the difference lies.

6. **differ about, differ with** – use "differ about" to state a point of difference; use "differ with" to indicate the other person with whom you differ about a certain issue.

7. **enter at, enter into** – use "enter at" for a specific place; use "enter into" to state an arrangement involving others.

8. **live at, live in, live on** – use "live at" to indicate a specific place such as a hotel; use "live in" to indicate a country, province, or town; use "live on" to state a street location or a specific type of location such as a farm.

Exercise C

Select the correct preposition for each sentence below from the choices in parentheses. Refer to the rules above to make your selection.

1. We walked _____ (in, into) the store from the street.

2. Linda, who was taller, _____ (differed with, differed from) her sister.

3. We _____ (entered at, entered into) the front door.

4. My uncle _____ (stays at, stays on) the Imperial Hotel.

5. The teacher divided the tasks _____ (between, among) all the students.

6. My friend was angry _____ (at, with) me.

7. _____ (Besides, Beside) my family, there will be no one else coming for dinner.

8. He _____ (entered at, entered into) an agreement with his parents to clean his room.

9. He rested _____ (besides, beside) the road before continuing his bike ride.

Exercise D

Choose the adverbs and adjectives from the word bank below and write them in the spaces provided to make a more interesting paragraph.

The School Picnic

generously   challenging   huge
lucky   dark   final   annual   silly
senior   fun   special   ferociously
suddenly   clear   wildly   slowly
quickly   hungry   early   local
gladly   sunny   blue   bright

Select the most obvious words first. Write your choices in pencil so that you can make changes if necessary. Some words are interchangeable.

Our 1._____ school picnic was scheduled for the 2._____ week in June. The 3._____ students were responsible for organizing the 4._____ event.

Fortunately, it was a 5._____ , 6._____ day. All the students in the school 7._____ assembled at the 8._____ park 9._____ in the morning. The first set of games, which included races, were very 10._____ . Some of the games such as the egg toss were 11._____ but 12._____ . The students 13._____ participated in hope of winning a special 14._____ ribbon.

When the games were finished, food was served to the 15._____ students. The teachers 16._____ prepared the barbecue to meet the 17._____ demand for food.

We were very 18._____ to have such great weather. The sky was 19._____ all day. 20._____ , just as we were getting ready to leave, a 21._____ thunder cloud drifted 22._____ overhead. In a matter of moments, the rain pelted down 23._____ . Screaming 24._____ , we ran for cover.

4 Understanding Verb Forms

Verb-Subject Agreement

A verb is a word that states the action performed by the subject in a sentence. The subject may be a noun, a pronoun, or a clause. Although there are numerous verb forms, verbs must agree in person and number with their subjects.

Verb-Subject **Agreement**

Exercise A

In each sentence below, place the correct verb that agrees in person and number with the subject of the sentence.

1. She _____ (makes, make) her bed each morning before school.

2. The automobile _____ (need, needed) many repairs.

3. We _____ (wished, wishes) for good weather during our vacation.

4. The boys _____ (plays, play) football in the park.

5. The friend of the girls _____ (arrive, arrived) here yesterday.

6. Where _____ (is, are) the other twin brother?

7. The six fish _____ (cost, costs) more than twenty dollars.

Compound Subjects

If the compound subject has two different nouns joined by "and", then it should be treated as a plural subject; but, if the compound subject represents two items that go together to make a single unit, then it is treated as a singular subject.

Exercise B

Singular subjects connected by "or" or "nor" take a singular verb.

1. Neither Sharon nor Victoria _____ (is, are) going to see the movie.

2. Singing and dancing _____ (requires, require) a lot of energy.

3. Tea and toast _____ (are, is) a simple refreshment.

4. He and I _____ (is, are) playing on the same team.

5. Apple pie and ice cream _____ (is, are) one of her favourite treats.

6. Philip or Craig _____ (play, plays) the piano.

When a compound subject is made up of both a singular and a plural noun separated by "either – or" or "neither – nor", place the plural noun second and make the verb agree.

7. Either John or his friends _____ (has, have) the proper address for the party.

8. Neither her mother nor her sisters _____ (realize, realizes) what time it is.

Fractions and Nouns of Quantity

With fractions, the verb agrees with the noun (object of the preposition) in the phrase. If measures of quantity, distance, time, and amount are meant to be single units, use a singular verb.

Exercise C

1. One quarter of the students _____ (was, were) late for school.

2. Half of the highway _____ (were, was) closed for repair.

3. Thirty dollars _____ (have, has) been put aside for the cost of the food.

4. 18 years _____ (are, is) a long time to be in school.

5. Two years _____ (have, has) gone by since the last time I met her.

6. 30% of the people living in the town _____ (is, are) over sixty.

Indefinite Pronoun Agreement

Because indefinite pronouns do not refer to specific things, it can be difficult to decide whether they require a singular or plural verb.

Examples: anyone, everyone, no one, somebody (singular)

both, few, many, several (plural)

all, any, most, more, none, some, enough (singular or plural, depending on the noun they refer to)

Exercise D

1. Many _____ (are, is) called, but few _____ (is, are) chosen.

2. All of the food _____ (were, was) eaten.

3. Nobody _____ (wants, want) to be the first to speak out.

4. None of the boys _____ (wants, want) to be the captain of the team.

5. Everyone _____ (agree, agrees) to help clean up the mess.

6. Somebody _____ (has, have) told her the secret.

Active and Passive Verb Voice

The voice of a verb indicates whether the subject of the verb is the performer of the action of the verb, or whether the subject is the receiver of the action of the verb.

Examples: John threw the ball through the window.
The subject "John" is doing the throwing.

The ball was thrown through the window by John.
The subject "ball" is receiving the action.

Exercise E

Write "Active" or "Passive" after each sentence below.

1. The students enjoyed doing science experiments. _____

2. The game was played during the lunch hour. _____

3. She called her friend on the telephone. _____

4. The teacher is being asked to teach at another school. _____

5. A party is being organized by the students. _____

A **Transitive Verb** directs action towards a noun or pronoun. This noun or pronoun that is the receiver of the action of the verb is called an object.

Example: Jake (subject) dropped (verb) the book (object) on the floor.
"The book" is the receiver of the action of the verb.

Exercise F

Underline the transitive verbs in the following sentences and place parentheses ( ) around the objects of the verbs in the sentences.

Remember: The direct object answers the question "what" or "whom".

1. They finished their homework before going out to play.

2. He sailed his boat across the lake.

3. Whenever it is cold outside, she wears a heavy sweater.

4. If we don't play well, we will lose the game.

5. Are you eating your dinner now?

6. He ate meat and potatoes for supper.

An **Intransitive Verb** indicates an action not directed towards an object. An intransitive verb does not have an object. A verb is also intransitive if the intended or implied object is left out.

Examples: The children played happily in the park.
The teacher asked.

Exercise 4

Indicate whether the verbs in the sentences below are transitive or intransitive by placing "TR" or "INT" in the spaces provided. Underline the verbs.

In the first sentence on the left, there is no object receiving the action of the verb "played". In the second example, the object is implied but not stated.

1. We watched the baseball game from across the street. _____

2. The ball was thrown from the pitcher to the catcher. _____

3. The volleyball team won the tournament championship. _____

4. The fans watched intensely as the home team lost the game. _____ _____

5. When the relatives arrived, they unpacked their bags. _____ _____

6. The girls sang in the school choir and the spectators were delighted by the music. _____ _____

7. The students, with the help of their teacher, were successful in school. _____

CHALLENGE

Change the verb voice in each sentence below.

1. The children gathered flowers from the garden.

    _____

2. She met her friends at the bus stop.

    _____

3. The dog ate the scraps on the table.

    _____

4. The children were entertained by the clown.

    _____

If the voice is active, change it to passive; if the voice is passive, change it to the active voice.

5 Verb Tenses

The Present Tense

Simple Present and Progressive Present

The simple present includes events that are happening at the time of speaking as well as events that go on all the time.

Simple: He **lives** in Toronto.
Progressive: He **is living** in Toronto.

Present Perfect Progressive

This verb tense indicates action that is going on at present but started in the past.

Example: He **has been living** in Toronto.

Note: The present perfect tense uses auxiliary (helper) words "has been".

Exercise A

Change the verb in each sentence to the tense required in parentheses.

1. Paula walks to school instead of taking the bus. (Progressive present)

   _____

2. I had a new bicycle. (Simple present)

   _____

3. She is walking her dog in the park. (Present perfect progressive)

   _____

4. We were swimming in the lake. (Present perfect progressive)

   _____

5. My friends and I planned to have a party. (Progressive present)

   _____

6. My dog will chase the ball. (Present perfect progressive)

   _____

The Past Tense

Simple Past

The simple past refers to events that took place in the past. These events have been completed and do not extend to the present.

Example: The team **won** the final game.

Past Progressive

This tense indicates actions that were continuing or actions that occurred in the past but with limitations.

Example: The team **was winning** the game the last time we checked the score.

Past Perfect

This tense indicates past action that was completed by a certain time in the past or before another past action occurred.

Example: The team **had won** the game by the time we checked the score.

Past Perfect Progressive

This tense indicates continuing action in the past that began before a certain time, or before another action in the past occurred.

Example: The team **had been winning** the game until the other team scored a goal.

Exercise B

In each of the following sentences, change the verb in parentheses to the tense indicated.

1. Children _____ (play) on the swings there. (Past progressive)

2. The sun _____ (shine) on the flowers. (Simple past)

3. The news _____ (arrive) by Internet transmission. (Past perfect progressive)

4. Many people _____ (watch) the World Cup. (Past perfect)

5. His cousin _____ (visit) them in January. (Past perfect progressive)

6. He _____ (help) his father cut the grass. (Simple past)

7. The students _____ (do) their homework together. (Past perfect)

8. The phone rang when we _____ (have) dinner. (Past progressive)

9. No one _____ (try) that before. (Past perfect)

The Future Tense

Simple Future

This tense indicates action that will occur in the future.

Example: They **will work** hard in school.

Future Progressive

This tense indicates continuing action in the future.

Example: They **will be working** hard in school.

Future Perfect

This tense indicates action that will be completed in the future before a certain time or before a certain event.

Example: They **will have worked** hard in school before the end of the year arrives.

Future Perfect Progressive

This tense indicates continuing action that will be completed by a certain time in the future.

Example: They **will have been working** hard in school by the time school ends.

Exercise C

In each of the following sentences, change the verb in parentheses to the tense indicated.

1. We _____ (wait) for the train to enter the terminal. (Simple future)

2. The game _____ (is played) in bad weather. (Future perfect progressive)

3. Sophia _____ (give) a lot of her time to help the school. (Future perfect)

4. I _____ (go) to see my grandfather play in a bowling tournament. (Simple future)

5. Many people _____ (want) to listen to the politician speak. (Future perfect)

6. We _____ (watch out) for our friends who are arriving any time now. (Simple future)

7. Our teacher _____ (congratulate) us on our success. (Future perfect progressive)

8. The distance runner _____ (pace) himself during the race. (Future perfect)

Complete the following sentences in your own way using the appropriate verb tenses.

1. When he saw me, _____

2. Fred usually walks to school, but yesterday _____

3. For the past month, our teacher _____

4. If you happen to see Jason, please _____

5. Next week, all of us _____

6. By the time the rain stopped, _____

7. Do you know where my folder is? I _____

8. The door closed just as we _____

CHALLENGE

Dad and I <u>went</u> to a ball game last weekend. We <u>were</u> late because of the traffic. By the time we <u>reached</u> the stadium, the rival team <u>had scored</u> twice. How disappointing! Next time, we <u>will make</u> sure to allow more time for traffic.

Write a short paragraph making use of three of the tenses you have learnt.

_____

_____

_____

_____

_____

_____

6 The Sentence and Its Parts

Subject and Predicate

A sentence is made up of words that express a complete thought. Basically, a sentence is divided into two parts: the subject and the predicate.

The subject contains a noun or pronoun that usually performs the action of the verb in the sentence.

Included in the subject of a sentence are the modifiers of the subject – descriptive words such as adjectives and adjective phrases.

The predicate of a sentence contains the verb (action word) and its modifiers – descriptive words such as adverbs and adverb phrases.

Exercise A

Draw a line to separate the subject and the predicate in each sentence below. Place parentheses ( ) around the modifiers of both the subject and the verb. Include adjective and adverb phrases with your modifiers.

1. The (old) man│walked (slowly) (down the street).

2. The cute kitten was playing with a ball of wool.

3. The old building was being demolished by the wrecking crew.

4. The uncertain weather caused a delay in our plans.

5. Water-skiing is difficult if you are a beginner.

6. We walked two miles to get to town.

7. The hot sun shines brightly in the sky.

8. I was laughing at the clown.

Articles are classified as adjectives but they do not describe a noun in the same detailed way that an adjective would. "A", "an", and "the" are articles also known as noun determiners. They help us distinguish which nouns are being referred to in a sentence. There are two types of articles: "definite" and "indefinite".

Example: He took **the** ball from **a** cupboard.

"The" is a definite article because it tells exactly which ball was taken. "A" describes "cupboard" but it is an indefinite article because it doesn't state which cupboard is being referred to.

Use "a" before a noun beginning with a consonant, "an" before a noun beginning with a vowel, and "the" to indicate a specific noun.

Exercise B

Place the proper article before the noun in each of the following sentences.

1. _____ (a, an) apple a day keeps the doctor away.

2. He placed _____ (the , a) books that he had finished reading on his shelf.

3. Which of _____ (an, a, the) players will score the winning goal?

4. Paul is _____ (an, a) enthusiastic student.

5. Sophia felt _____ (the, a) sudden urge to eat chocolate.

6. This is _____ (a, an, the) great day to get outdoors.

 Direct and Indirect Objects

A direct object is the receiver of the action of a transitive verb.
An indirect object is a noun or pronoun that tells to whom or for whom the action of the verb is directed.

Example: John gave Susan his book.
"John" is the subject of the sentence and the performer of the action.
The verb "gave" represents the action (transitive) in the sentence.
The "book" is the direct object that receives the action of the verb "gave".
"Susan" is the indirect object because the action of the verb is directed to her.

Exercise C

Underline the direct objects and place parentheses ( ) around the indirect objects in the sentences below.

1. Paula bought her lunch at the restaurant.

2. The teacher gave the students an assignment.

3. His coach gave him a warm welcome when he came off the ice.

4. The parents gave their children treats for lunch.

5. She told her friend the truth about what happened.

6. Jeremy took all his gym equipment home to be washed.

7. The driver told the passengers the good news.

8. The clerk sold us a ticket to the concert.

9. Our teacher prepared us for an important literacy test.

Object of a Preposition

The noun following a preposition in a phrase is an object of the preposition.

Example: The student sat **in** his **desk**.

The phrase "in his desk" is introduced by the preposition "in". The noun "desk" is the object of the preposition "in".

There are 10 objects of prepositions below; one sentence has 3 objects!

Exercise D

Underline the objects of the prepositions in the following sentences.

1. In the morning, we prepared to leave for school.

2. Into the cool water dove the overheated children.

3. We rowed our boat far from the shore.

4. The students in our class prepared to face the chilly weather at recess.

5. Over the hill and beyond the horizon, the sun set in the ocean.

6. The cat ventured into the night under the moonlight.

Other Predicate Complements

A **Predicate Nominative** is a noun or noun substitute that follows an intransitive verb and refers to the subject.

Example: The winner was **Paul**.

A **Predicate Adjective** is an adjective that follows an intransitive verb and describes the subject.

Example: Paul is **tall**.

Exercise E

Identify each italicized word in the following sentences by placing "A" for predicate nominative or "B" for predicate adjective in the space provided.

1. Although she didn't succeed, this student is still very *clever*.   _____

2. Paul is the *creator* of the new game that we all play at recess time.   _____

3. She was *wise* because she prepared herself for whatever might happen.   _____

4. Richard was the *leader*; Brian was the *follower*.   _____   _____

5. The dessert was *delicious* but it was also *fattening*.　　　—— ——

6. Whenever we see her, she is always *happy*.　　　——

CHALLENGE

Indentify the parts of speech in each sentence. Choose from the parts of speech listed below for your answers. Write the letters in the parentheses.

The adverb and adjective phrases are underlined. Identify the type of phrase for each.

> **A.** article　**B.** noun　**C.** adjective　**D.** adjective phrase
> **E.** verb　**F.** adverb　**G.** direct object
> **H.** object of preposition　**I.** preposition　**J.** adverb phrase

1. The losing team shook hands <u>with the winners</u>.
   (　)(　　)(　　)(　　)(　　) (　　　　　　)

2. The students <u>of Maple Avenue school</u> collected money
   (　)(　　　　) (　　　　　　　　　) (　　　) (　　　)

   <u>for a charity</u>.
   (　　　　　)

3. An old friend <u>of mine</u> came <u>to my school</u> today <u>before noon</u>.
   (　)(　)(　　)(　　　)(　　)(　　　　　　)(　　)(　　　　　)

4. The man told me to go <u>over the hill</u> <u>to the little farm house</u>.
   (　)(　　)(　)(　)(　　)(　　　　　)(　　　　　　　　)

5. The boy <u>in blue jeans</u> is the cousin <u>of my friend</u>.
   (　)(　)(　　)(　　　　　)(　)(　)(　　)(　　　　)

6. Many students <u>of grade 3</u> are waiting excitedly <u>for the play</u> to start.
   (　　)(　　　)(　　　　)(　　　、　)(　　　　)(　　　　)(　)(　)

7. Christa is leaving Canada <u>for Japan</u> tonight.
   (　　　)(　　　)(　　　)(　　　)(　　)

7 Compound and Complex Sentences

> **Definitions**
>
> A **Simple Sentence** is made up of one subject and one verb.
>
> A **Compound Sentence** is made up of two or more simple sentences joined by a conjunction (and, if, but, or, so...) or by a semi-colon (;).

Exercise A

Complete the compound sentences with the simple sentences in the box. Use the correct conjunctions.

> Use each conjunction only once.

because   if

and   so

- • I study very hard for the test.
- • We could go out and play.
- • I saw a squirrel climb a tree.
- • We all played games.

1. I walked in the park _____

2. We did all our homework _____

3. Her birthday party was a lot of fun _____

4. I will receive a high mark in Science _____

The Subordinate Clause

A sentence is sometimes called an "independent clause" because a sentence is a complete thought and can stand on its own without needing more information to complete its meaning.

A subordinate clause is a "dependent clause" because it needs an independent clause to complete its meaning.

Like an independent clause (sentence), a subordinate clause has a noun and a verb. It has a connecting word or conjunction usually at the beginning.

Examples: 1. although I enjoy eating pizza
2. when I was walking home from school
3. after we watched the game on television

Did you notice that all of the clauses in the examples have nouns and verbs but are incomplete sentences because they do not give enough information?

Exercise B

After each sentence or clause below, state whether it is an independent clause (complete sentence) or a dependent clause (incomplete sentence) by placing "IC" for an independent clause or "DC" for a dependent clause in the space provided.

1. Winter is my favourite season of the year. _____

2. When summer arrives. _____

3. After the boys played baseball and put
    away the equipment. _____

4. Because it was a beautiful sunny day. _____

5. When are you leaving? _____

6. Look out, the shelf is falling! _____

7. Where does the new student live? _____

8. If you choose to play instead of work. _____

9. The girls beat the boys in the spelling contest. _____

10. When I get home from school. _____

11. Before he could have the chance to read
    the answers. _____

12. Give it to Daniel. _____

13. Unless you let me go with you. _____

14. He rode his bicycle to school every day. _____

Clauses and Phrases

There is difference between clauses and phrases.

A **phrase** is a group of words that does not have both a noun and a verb, and begins with a preposition (in, under, of...). A phrase describes either a noun or a verb.

Examples: in the box, under the table, behind the bookshelf, of the class, at the game...

A **clause** contains a noun and a verb, and begins with a subordinating conjunction (whenever, after, because...).

Exercise C

Identify each of the following groups of words as either a phrase or a subordinate clause. Write "phrase" or "clause" in the space provided. If you find a complete sentence, write the word "sentence".

There are three complete sentences. Did you find them?

1. Whenever I ask a question. _____
2. Towards the street corner. _____
3. They walked under the bridge. _____
4. If it rains this afternoon. _____
5. They play golf on Saturdays. _____
6. Nothing is better than a hot slice of pizza. _____
7. Below the window ledge. _____
8. Because they asked me to help them. _____

Adverbial and Adjectival Clauses

An **adverbial** clause does the same job as an adverb – it tells where or when the action of the verb takes place.

Example: We did not leave **until everyone boarded the bus**.
The clause "until everyone boarded the bus" tells when the action took place.

An **adjectival** clause does the work of an adjective – it gives information about a noun in the sentence.

Example: My friend Randall, **who lives in London, England**, sends me e-mail messages once a week.
The clause "who lives in London, England" describes Randall.

Exercise D

Indicate by writing ADV (adverbial) or ADJ (adjectival) in the space following each sentence the type of clause written in italics.

1. *Whenever they went on holiday*, they always spent too much money. _____

2. *After we had eaten our lunch*, we played soccer in the park. _____

3. The teams, *which were chosen by the teacher*, were fair. _____

4. *If I knew that you were coming over,* I would have stayed home. _____

5. He was the only one *who knew what we were supposed to do.* _____

6. I took the bus instead *because I did not have enough money.* _____

Exercise E

Add either an independent clause or a dependent clause to each partial sentence below to make a complete sentence.

1. Because the bus was delayed, _____

2. If you try your best, _____

3. The restaurant was empty even though _____

   _____

4. While we sat waiting for the movie to begin, _____

   _____

5. I was frightened on Halloween because _____

   _____

Exercise F

Write a brief descriptive story on "The Winning Goal" using subordinate clauses in your sentences. Try using these subordinating conjunctions in your sentences.

whenever	because	after	before	while	however

_____

_____

_____

_____

_____

Types of Nouns

Exercise A

Identify each of the following nouns: simple, proper, compound, and collective.

1. automobile _____
2. doctor _____
3. professor _____
4. fireplace _____
5. mother _____
6. group _____
7. City Hall _____
8. Calgary _____
9. flashlight _____
10. orchestra _____
11. family _____
12. crew _____
13. January _____
14. Doctor Jones _____

Noun Plurals

Exercise B

Write the plural form of the following nouns.

1. boat _____
2. ox _____
3. woman _____
4. coach _____
5. bush _____
6. hero _____
7. wife _____
8. knife _____
9. zoo _____
10. shoe _____
11. cliff _____
12. lady _____

Verbs to Nouns

Exercise C

Change each of the following verbs to its noun form.

1. bakes _____
2. creates _____
3. design _____
4. plays _____
5. thinks _____
6. swim _____
7. teach _____
8. help _____
9. plans _____
10. builds _____
11. speaks _____
12. lie _____

30

Pronouns

> A pronoun replaces a noun. A noun in a sentence that is replaced by a pronoun is called an antecedent.

Exercise D

For each of the following sentences, choose the correct pronoun to suit the antecedent.

1. The whole group of friends brought _____ (his, her, their) photos.
2. Paul and Peter were early because _____ (he, they, it) left ahead of the others.
3. We brought _____ (our, their) own food for the picnic.
4. My dog loves to play with _____ (its, his, her) rubber bone.
5. We asked _____ (those, them, him) if they would help us.
6. The children played with _____ (their, its, mine) toys by themselves.
7. I was hoping that the teacher would choose _____ (me, I) to be the class representative.

Types of Pronouns

> Do you remember the four types of pronouns: demonstrative, interrogative, relative, and reflexive?

Exercise E

In each of the following sentences, choose the correct pronoun and fill in the blanks. In the space following the sentence, state which type of pronoun it is.

1. _____ (what, which) of the children was crying?   _____
2. _____ (who, whose) will be our new teacher?   _____
3. Give _____ (those, that, them) pencils to the students.   _____
4. He brought a gift _____ (those, that) surprised everyone.   _____
5. The person _____ (who, whom) spoke out was embarrassed.   _____
6. She wore _____ (herself, themselves) out running too fast.   _____

Progress Test 1

Adverbs and Adjectives

Exercise F

Complete the following sentences with suitable adjectives or adverbs.

Adverbs describe verbs; adjectives describe nouns.

> loudly   completely   happily   cleverly   menacingly
> sly   tall   threatening   cheerful   frightened

1. The _____ , little boy called _____ for his mother.
2. The _____ tree shaded the flower garden _____ .
3. The _____ children played _____ in the playground.
4. The _____ , old fox hunted _____ for the unsuspecting mouse.
5. Dark, _____ clouds hovered _____ overhead.

Adjective and Adverb Phrases

Exercise G

Underline the adjective phrases and place parentheses ( ) around the adverb phrases in each sentence below.

Adjective and adverb phrases do the same work in a sentence as adverbs and adjectives.

1. The bird in the bush sang a song of the wild.
2. Under the carpet, he hid his gift of money.
3. In the middle of the night, it began raining.
4. The choir of St. Michael's sang in the church near the village.

Prepositions

Exercise H

Select the proper preposition and fill in the blank in each of the following sentences.

1. She had to decide _____ (among, between) the two choices.
2. He walked _____ (into, in) the house to get out of the cold.
3. My results are different _____ (with, from) the teacher's.
4. The children differed _____ (in, from) the choice of activity.
5. We couldn't agree _____ (to, on) where to go for the game.

Verb-Subject Agreement

Exercise I

Write the correct verb form in the space provided in each of the following sentences.

1. Neither of the girls _____ (wish, wishes) to participate in the choir.

2. Jamie and Andrew _____ (play, plays) on the same hockey team.

3. Peaches and cream _____ (is, are) her favourite dessert.

4. Neither the coach nor the swimmers _____ (wants, want) to practise in the lake.

5. Running and jumping _____ (makes, make) up the hurdle event.

6. Susan or Sharon _____ (choose, chooses) between the participants.

7. One quarter of the students _____ (write, writes) the test in the classroom.

Active and Passive Voice

> With an active voice, the subject performs the action. With the passive voice, the subject is the receiver of the action.

Exercise J

Change the following sentences from active voice to passive, or from passive to active.

1. The car was driven by Patricia's father.

   _____

2. That picture on the wall was drawn by me.

   _____

3. Sam's mother made the birthday cake.

   _____

4. We planted the tree in the backyard.

   _____

5. The alarm was set off by the naughty children.

   _____

Transitive and Intransitive Verbs

Transitive verbs direct action towards an object (noun or pronoun) in a sentence. Intransitive verbs do not direct their action to an object.

Exercise K

Identify each of the following sentences as being transitive or intransitive.

1. She invited all her classmates to a barbecue at her home. _____
2. They waited for a long time for the bus. _____
3. Peter phoned his friend after dinner. _____
4. The team was disappointed because they didn't play well. _____
5. Irene made a card for her mother. _____
6. She left without the teacher's permission. _____

Direct and Indirect Objects

A direct object receives the action of the verb. An indirect object tells to whom or to what the action of the verb is directed.

Exercise L

Underline the direct objects and place parentheses ( ) around the indirect objects in each sentence below. Identify the type of object by writing "D" or "I" in the space provided.

Some sentences may have both types of objects. List them in the order they appear.

1. He chased his dog around the yard. _____
2. She gave her the address to her house. _____ _____
3. The rain soaked the flowers in the yard. _____
4. The teacher gave the students homework. _____ _____
5. She called her friend to invite her to go swimming. _____
6. He asked me to go with him. _____
7. His father bought him a new bike. _____ _____

Objects of Prepositions

The noun following a preposition in a phrase is called the object of the preposition.

Exercise M

Underline the objects of the prepositions only. Do not underline direct or indirect objects in the sentences.

One sentence has 2 objects of prepositions.

1. In the moonlight, we could see quite well.
2. The chair was tucked under the table.
3. After the rainfall, the sun came out.
4. He slept throughout the movie.
5. Over the hill and beyond the farmhouse, we found the lost sheep.

Compound and Complex Sentences

A compound sentence has two simple sentences joined by a conjunction. A complex sentence has a principal clause and a subordinate clause.

Exercise N

Change the simple sentences into compound or complex sentences.

1. The children stopped playing. They were too tired.

   _____

2. I like mangoes. I don't like bananas.

   _____

3. Jason is short. He can play basketball well.

   _____

4. We can go there by subway. We can go there by bus.

   _____

5. I will tell you. You don't tell anyone else.

   _____

8 Verbal, Participle, and Infinitive Phrases

Verbals are verb forms that do not act as verbs in sentences. Instead, they function as nouns, adjectives, and adverbs.

There are three kinds of verbals: participle, gerund, and infinitive.

Participles have been reviewed in a previous unit.

Gerunds are verbals that act as nouns. They look like participles because they end in "ing". Gerunds are often the subject or the object in a sentence.

Example (1): **Skiing** is fun. The word "skiing" is a gerund acting as the subject of the sentence. It is the gerund form of the verb "ski".

Example (2): She enjoys **swimming**. The word "swimming" is a gerund acting as the object of the sentence. It is what is being enjoyed.

Exercise A

Fill in each blank with the gerund form of the verb in parentheses. Circle "Subj." or "Obj." at the end of the sentence to state whether the gerund is the subject or object.

1. _____ (jump) over a puddle can be risky. **Subj.** **Obj.**

2. _____ (fall) from your bicycle can be painful. **Subj.** **Obj.**

3. Paul loves _____ (chew) bubble gum. **Subj.** **Obj.**

4. _____ (win) the game was the only thing that mattered to him. **Subj.** **Obj.**

5. She enjoyed _____ (sip) her tea and _____ (eat) cake. **Subj.** **Obj.**

6. _____ (sing) and _____ (dance) are her favourite activities. **Subj.** **Obj.**

7. Jason is keen on _____ (make) models. **Subj.** **Obj.**

8. Grandpa likes _____ (watch) old movies. **Subj.** **Obj.**

9. _____ (play) street hockey is what they like to do on weekends. **Subj.** **Obj.**

The **Infinitive** is formed by adding the word "to" to a verb. For example, the infinitive form of "run" would be "to run".

Note: "To be" is the infinitive form of the familiar verbs: is, are, was, were.
The infinitive can play the role of a noun, adjective, or an adverb in a sentence.

Example (1): He wanted **to play**.
"To play" is acting as a noun (object). It is what was wanted.

Example (2): There was no time **to work**.
"To work" is acting as an adjective telling what kind of time it is.

Example (3): He was prepared **to clean** the car.
"To clean" is acting as an adverb explaining how he was prepared.

Exercise B

Underline the infinitives in the following sentences and state whether they are acting as nouns, adjectives, or adverbs. Circle your choices.

1. To fly across the sky is thrilling.   **noun**   **adjective**   **adverb**

2. He wanted to speak to his teacher.   **noun**   **adjective**   **adverb**

3. To write a letter is sometimes difficult.   **noun**   **adjective**   **adverb**

4. He was ready to play the hockey game.   **noun**   **adjective**   **adverb**

5. They were happy to come to the party.   **noun**   **adjective**   **adverb**

Present and Past Participles

Participles function as adjectives in a sentence.

Example: The **winning** team received the trophy.
"Winning" is the present participle form of "win" and describes the noun "team".
Therefore it is acting as an adjective.

Exercise C

#3 has two participles.

Underline the participle in each of the following sentences and write the noun that it describes in the space.

1. He woke up the sleeping giant.   _____

2. He swallowed his chewing gum.   _____

3. The swaying branches made rustling noises.   _____

4. The carrying case was handy for travelling.   _____

5. The cutting edge of the knife was very sharp.   _____

A **Participle Phrase** acts as an adjective and begins with a participle.

Example (1): **Standing in the rain**, I got very wet.

"Standing" is the participle, and "Standing in the rain" is the participle phrase. This participle phrase is an adjective phrase describing the pronoun "I".

Example (2): **Thrilled at winning the game**, the players celebrated.

"Thrilled" is the participle, and "Thrilled at winning the game" is the participle phrase. This participle phrase is an adjective phrase describing the noun "players".

Exercise D

Underline the participle phrase in each of the following sentences. Write the noun that it describes in the space following the sentence.

1. Waiting for a long time, the lady read her book. _____

2. The old man climbing the stairs was out of breath. _____

3. Thrilled with the outcome, the winner accepted the praise. _____

4. The students playing in the gym wore running shoes. _____

5. Worried that he would be late for school, the boy ran all the way. _____

6. The orchestra playing a classical tune entertained everyone. _____

7. He followed his friends, hoping not to get lost. _____

8. Delighted with the cake that she baked, the girl gave everyone a piece. _____

9. Frightened by the bulldog, the children ran away from the backyard. _____

10. The woman carrying an umbrella walked slowly in the rain. _____

11. Hearing the bad news, the actress broke into tears. _____

12. The puppy chasing the birds is very cute. _____

13. Surrounded by police, the robber couldn't get away. _____

Exercise E

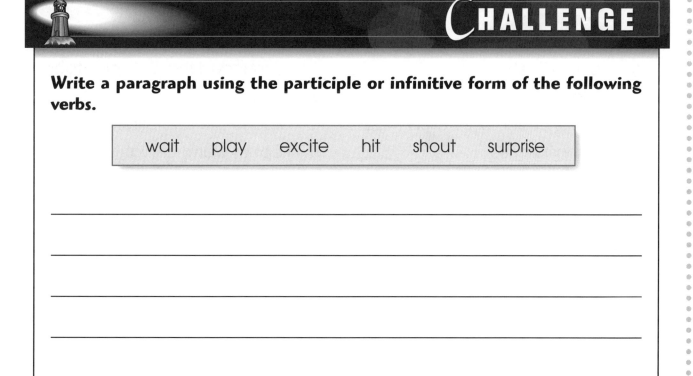

Rewrite each of the sentences below replacing the italicized noun (subject) with a gerund or an infinitive.

1. *Baseball* is fun.

   Playing baseball is fun. (gerund) or _____

   To play baseball is fun. (infinitive)

2. A *fall* from a horse can be dangerous. (change to a gerund)

   _____

3. A *loss* in the first game upset the players. (change to a gerund)

   _____

4. *Laughter* makes you feel much better when you are sad.
   (change to an infinitive)

   _____

5. He loves *singing* in the shower. (change to an infinitive)

   _____

6. *Exercise* is good for both the mind and the body. (change to a gerund)

   _____

CHALLENGE

Write a paragraph using the participle or infinitive form of the following verbs.

| wait | play | excite | hit | shout | surprise |

_____

_____

_____

_____

_____

9 Phrases – Noun, Gerund, Appositive, Absolute

A **Noun Phrase** is made up of a noun and all its modifiers. A noun phrase can be a subject, object, or a sentence complement (following the verb to be).

Example (Subject):   **Healthy, green salad** is served in the cafeteria.
The noun phrase "Healthy, green salad" is acting as subject of the verb "is".

Example (Object):   They eat **healthy, green salad**.
The noun phrase "healthy, green salad" is acting as object of the verb "eat".

Example (Complement):   A piece of fruit is **a healthy snack**.
The noun phrase "a healthy snack" is the complement to the verb "is".

Exercise A

The noun phrase does not have to be the subject of the sentence.

Match the noun phrases with the sentence remainders by writing letters in the blanks. Then write sentences with them.

Column A

1. fine, colourful silk _____
2. hot, spicy sauce _____
3. expensive, costume jewellery _____
4. scary, ghost stories _____
5. bright, colourful flags _____
6. warm, fuzzy blankets _____

Column B

A. surrounded the Olympic Stadium
B. she wore
C. around the campfire, they told
D. kept us warm all night long.
E. was used to make neckties.
F. was spread on the pizza.

1. _____
2. _____
3. _____
4. _____
5. _____
6. _____

A **Gerund Phrase** is made up of a gerund and its modifiers, objects or complements. A gerund phrase can act as subject of the verb, complement of the verb "to be", direct or indirect object, and object of a preposition.

Rules of Use

A. **Subject**: **Playing football** is a game we all enjoy.

B. **Object**: He likes **playing football** with his friends after school.

C. **Complement**: The greatest excitement is **playing football**.

D. **Object of a Preposition**: He was very good at **throwing a football**. "At" is the preposition; "throwing a football" is object of the preposition.

Exercise B

Underline the gerund phrase in each of the sentences below and write the letter from the rules above that corresponds to the use of the gerund phrase.

1. Laughing out loud disturbed the people in the audience. _____

2. She enjoyed playing the piano in front of a crowd. _____

3. By keeping the news a secret, she gained their trust. _____

4. He practised running around the track. _____

5. Sweeping the floors took a long time. _____

6. Happiness is flying a kite. _____

7. Making muffins is an easy job. _____

Exercise C

Complete the sentences below with a gerund phrase of your own.

1. _____ was a dangerous task.

2. They enjoyed _____ .

3. Danger is _____ .

4. From _____ , they were tired.

5. After _____ , everyone went home.

6. _____ was so much fun.

7. _____ can't solve the problem.

8. I'll never forget _____ .

The Appositive Phrase

A noun phrase that gives another name for the noun or pronoun directly before it in a sentence is called an appositive phrase.

Example: Wayne Gretsky, **a great hockey player**, attended the celebrity banquet.

The phrase "a great hockey player" is the appositive to the proper noun "Wayne Gretsky".

Exercise D

Underline the appositive phrases in the following sentences and add commas where necessary.

1. The cottage we rented the one with the large front porch has a nice beach.

2. That dog the one with the bushy tail belongs to him.

3. He wanted a bicycle one with racing wheels for his birthday.

4. He chose the first seat the one near the window because it had a view.

5. His sister the one in grade three is waiting for him at the front door of the school.

6. He drove the other car the green convertible to work every day.

7. The players those who showed up on time got the most playing time.

8. Snowboarding a sport for the young has become very popular.

9. Health the thing we all desire can be achieved by eating properly.

10. Fatigue the state of exhaustion followed her completion of the marathon.

Exercise E

Form your own appositive phrases. Be sure to include modifying words.

1. The new teacher, _____ , drives a very old car.

2. Chocolate cake, _____ , is delicious with ice cream.

3. We enjoy going to the beach, _____ .

4. He caught the ball, _____ .

5. The highway, _____ , is the route we always take.

6. My neighbour, _____ , borrowed our lawn mower.

7. I like the new boy, _____ .

8. The video game, _____ , is exciting and challenging.

An **Absolute Phrase** is made up of a noun or pronoun and a participle with objects and modifiers. An absolute phrase modifies the entire sentence rather than just a particular word. It may appear anywhere in a sentence and is set off from the sentence by commas.

Examples: The fans cheered the team, **arms waving madly in the air**.
My fear finally controlled, I entered the dentist office.

The boldfaced words above are absolute phrases because they modify the entire sentences.

Exercise F

Underline the absolute phrases in the following sentences and add commas where necessary.

1. The children are fully entertained the clown having made funny balloons for everyone.

2. He ran out of the house his lunch being left behind.

3. He roared down the ice everyone trying to catch him.

4. The ice cream melted chocolate spilling everywhere.

5. The teacher handed out the report cards students waiting anxiously.

6. They lined up for the penalty shot soccer fans standing motionless.

7. People running everywhere the rainstorm unleashed a heavy downpour.

8. Fans lining up for hours the tickets for the rock concert finally went on sale.

Exercise G

Put the absolute phrases with the sentences that they are best suited to modify.

> skiers dotting the hillside   the dog sitting up begging
> the end of the game coming near   the runners taking their marks
> the contestants holding their breath

1. He held up the piece of hamburger, _____ .

2. The starter gun was about to go off, _____ .

3. _____ , the winner was announced.

4. _____ , the racers swerved in and out of the people.

5. _____ , they made one last effort to get the tying goal.

10 Run-On Sentences and Sentence Combining

A **Run-on Sentence** occurs when two sentences are joined together without proper punctuation or connecting words.

Example: I was expecting him earlier he must be delayed.

There are actually two sentences here: "I was expecting him earlier" and "He must be late". This run-on sentence should become two sentences by placing a period after the word "earlier" and placing a capital on the word "he".

In some cases, one part of the run-on sentence can be made into a subordinate clause.

Example: It was raining we used an umbrella.
This run-on sentence can be changed to: Because it was raining, we used an umbrella.

Exercise A

Correct the following run-on sentences by either changing them to two sentences or by making one part a subordinate clause.

1. Lunch was ready we ate in the kitchen.

   _____

2. The door is wide open someone must be home.

   _____

3. He has cut his foot he put a bandage on it.

   _____

4. The buzzer went the game was over.

   _____

5. She read the book it was about a mystery it took place in England.

   _____

6. The train arrived at the station it was half an hour late.

   _____

7. The weather was fine we had a game of baseball.

   _____

8. It was breezy our kites flew high in the sky.

   _____

Sentence Combining

The following short sentences can be combined to make longer sentences.

Exercise B

Combine each group of sentences into one sentence.

Remember to use conjunctions and subordinating conjunctions to create longer, more detailed sentences.

1. The cat mewed. The cat was hungry. The cat wanted milk.

   _____

2. The car was new. The car was shiny. The car was red.

   _____

3. He was a student. His school was St. Patrick's. He was in grade four.

   _____

4. She wore a coat. The coat was yellow. The coat was a ski jacket.

   _____

5. You should answer questions. You should raise your hand.

   _____

6. There was homework. The homework was mathematics. The homework was plenty.

   _____

7. The game was delayed. The game was baseball. The delay was because of rain.

   _____

8. The children participated in a race. The race was 100 metres. The race was in the schoolyard.

   _____

Exercise C

Join the most obvious ones first.

Choose a sentence from Column A that could be combined with a sentence from Column B. Write each new sentence in the space provided.

Column A	Column B
1. The mouse was frightened.	• She thought that she was lost.
2. The snow was like powder.	• He was locked out of the house.
3. The bird built a nest.	• They ate peanuts and cracker jacks.
4. He couldn't find his key.	• The cat was ready to pounce.
5. The little girl was crying.	• There was a break in the game.
6. They sailed on an ocean liner.	• The skiing was excellent.
7. They went to the baseball game.	• The sun came up.
8. The dresser drawers were full.	• It used twigs and bits of straw.
9. The players drank water.	• They had a wonderful vacation.
10. The morning dew melted.	• There was not enough room for his clothes.

1. _____

2. _____

3. _____

4. _____

5. _____

6. _____

7. _____

8. _____

9. _____

10. _____

Exercise D

Below is a passage containing short, choppy sentences. Combine the sentences that are common in topic. Rewrite the new paragraph in the space below.

Before you start combining the sentences, draw a line separating the sentences into groups that have common topics. Add words as needed. Change some phrases to adjectives. Avoid repeating words.

The Air Canada Centre is a large sports facility. The Air Canada Centre is in Toronto. The Air Canada Centre is downtown. Building of the centre started in 1997. Building of the centre was finished in 1999. The Air Canada Centre is home to the Toronto Maple Leafs. The Air Canada Centre is home to the Toronto Raptors. The first game played there was hockey. The first game was between the Toronto Maple Leafs and the Montreal Canadiens. The first hockey game was on February 20, 1999. The first Raptor game played in the Air Canada Centre was on February 21, 1999. The first Raptor game played there was against the Vancouver Grizzlies. Often there are special events going on there. There are meetings there. There are concerts there. There are community events there. The Air Canada Centre has seats. It has 19,800 seats for basketball games. It has 18,800 seats for hockey games.

_____

_____

_____

_____

_____

_____

_____

_____

_____

_____

11 Punctuation (1)

Sentence Types

A **declarative** sentence simply states a fact. It ends with a period (**.**).

An **imperative** sentence gives a command. It ends with a period (**.**).

An **interrogative** sentence asks a question. It ends with a question mark (**?**).

An **exclamatory** sentence makes a strong statement. It ends with an exclamation mark (**!**).

Exercise A

Punctuate each of the following sentences. Write the type of sentence in the space provided.

1. Look out _____

2. What time is it _____

3. It was an unusually hot day _____

4. What a hot day _____

5. Never do that again _____

6. Do as you are told _____

7. Help _____

8. It was nice of him to offer his help even though he was busy _____

9. Do you know which team got the champion in yesterday's match _____

An **Apostrophe** (**'**) is used to show possession of a noun. It is also used to indicate that one or more letters are missing from a word or that one or more numbers are missing from a number.

Example (1): missing number – He played in the '99 Stanley Cup finals.
The apostrophe replaces the numbers "19" in 1999.

Example (2): contraction – We didn't stop for lunch today.
The apostrophe replaces the letter "o" in the word "not".

Example (3): possession – This book is Susie's.
The apostrophe before the "s" shows possession.

Note: It is easy to confuse "its" and "it's".

"Its" is the possessive form of "it".

"It's" is the contracted form of "it is".

Exercise B

Complete the Contraction Chart. Fill in either the contraction or the expanded form of each word in the blank space.

	Expanded	Contracted
1.	could not	
2.	would not	
3.		I'd
4.	do not	
5.	cannot	
6.		you'll
7.	does not	
8.		he'd
9.	he has	
10.	should not	
11.		let's
12.	will not	
13.	is not	
14.		I've
15.	must not	

Possessives

1. Add an "s" to a singular noun to form the possessive case.
   Example: This was the cat**'s** collar.
2. If a plural noun does not end in "s", add "'s" to form the possessive case.
   Example: The children**'s** playground is behind the building.
3. Add only an apostrophe to plural nouns that end in "s".
   Example: The clowns**'** costumes were very colourful.
4. To singular nouns that end in "s", add "'s".
   Example: Dickens**'s** novels were written many years ago.
   Although "Dickens" ends in an "s", it is a singular proper noun.

Note: Possessive pronouns do not require possessive endings.

Make each word below possessive and rewrite it in the space provided. Write the rule # in the parentheses following each word.

1. people _____ ( )   2. person _____ ( )

3. women _____ ( )   4. boys _____ ( )

5. players _____ ( )   6. boy _____ ( )

7. hers _____ ( )   8. class _____ ( )

9. Keats _____ ( )   10. geese _____ ( )

11. children _____ ( )   12. Dennis _____ ( )

13. babies _____ ( )   14. cat _____ ( )

 CHALLENGE

Each sentence below has missing apostrophes. Place a line through each word missing the apostrophe. Make the correction directly above it.

> The number in parentheses at the end of each sentence tells you how many apostrophes are missing in each sentence.

1. Pauls coat wasnt left in the cloakroom. (2)

2. Its two oclock but it isnt too late to go out and play. (3)

3. I cant find my picture showing my championship team of 98. (2)

4. The bike was Susans but it wasnt the right size for her. (2)

5. Be very quiet and shell never know we were here. (1)

6. Lets not play tricks on him because it isnt nice. (2)

7. We woke Pauls dog because its time for its walk. (2)

8. Id have waited for you but you took too long. (1)

9. Dont forget to bring Louiss book with you. (2)

10. Whats the matter with your dog? (1)

Colons

1. Use a colon to introduce a list of items.

   Example: The following are John's favourite sports**:** baseball, basketball, tennis, and golf.

2. Use a colon to separate hours from minutes when using numbers to state time.

   Examples: 4**:**30 p.m.   11**:**01 a.m.

3. Use a colon to separate long quotations.

4. Use a colon to introduce an explanation.

   Example: Hockey equipment is necessary**:** a helmet, a face mask, chin pads, and shoulder pads.

Exercise D

Insert a colon where necessary in the following passage.

There are six colons missing.

The Camping Trip

The day arrived for our camping trip. We packed the following items a tent, a flashlight, a sleeping bag, and a cooler. Our guide gave us this important advice do not leave food around the tent after dark. He also explained "It is important to respect nature and the animals of the woodlands. Remember, you are visiting their territory. Treat it as if it was your own." We left home at 630 a.m. and arrived at the campsite at 1100. It took nearly two hours to set up camp because we had to take care of the following duties clearing the site, hammering in the tent pegs, fetching water, and setting up a campfire.

12 Punctuation (2)

The Comma – Rules of Use

1. Commas are used to separate three or more items in a list.

   Example: At the zoo they saw lions, tigers, elephants, and giraffes.

2. Commas are used to separate phrases and clauses in a series.

   Example: He promised to come home after school, cut the grass, and clean out the garage.

   The above example shows that clauses need to be separated when they are presented as a list of things to do.

3. Commas are used to set off the person you are talking to.

   Example: John, hand me that wrench.

4. Commas are used to separate the name of a city and a province, and between the day and the year of a date.

   Example: They moved to Toronto, Ontario on July 12, 2001.

Add commas where necessary. Place the rule number for the comma use in each sentence in the space provided.

> The number in parentheses at the end of the sentence tells you how many commas are needed in each sentence.

1. She wanted to finish school to go to college and to get a good job. (2)   _____

2. We worked ate slept and awoke the next day before they arrived. (3)   _____

3. We visited our relatives in Saskatoon Alberta. (1)   _____

4. His birthday was August 14 1992. (1)   _____

5 We ate soup sandwiches cake and ice cream for lunch. (3)   _____

6. Dad will you drive me to my friend's house? (1)   _____

7. Playing hockey going skiing and snowboarding are my favourite things to do. (2)   _____

8. The Raptors the Leafs and the Argos all play in Toronto Ontario. (3)   _____

Direct quotations are set off from the rest of the sentences by a comma following the last word before the quotation. If the quotation comes first, the comma is placed after the last word of the quotation.

Examples: His friend said, "Can you come to the movies with me?"

"I'm going to a movie," his friend said.

Note: If the quotation is followed by a question mark or an exclamation mark, no comma will follow.

Examples: "Where are you going?" he asked.

"Leave me alone!" he screamed.

Exercise B

Place a comma where necessary in the following sentences.

> There are only 6 commas needed in the sentences below.

1. "What do you want to eat for supper?" his mother asked.

2. "I wish we had school during the summer" said Susan.

3. "Don't touch that wire!" screamed the electrician.

4. "Do you have any apples pears or oranges?" asked the lady.

5. "Be careful!" he shouted. "There are snakes spiders and rats in the pit."

6. "We have to go now" Danny said.

Commas and Subordinate (Dependent) Clauses

Remember, a dependent clause is a group of words that has a noun and a verb, but depends on an independent clause to complete its meaning. A comma separates the dependent clause from the independent clause when the dependent clause appears first in a sentence.

Exercise C

Underline the dependent clause and add a comma if one is needed.

1. While he was walking home he saw a dog chase a cat.

2. Susan and Julie were excited while they cheered at the hockey game.

3. After they watched the movie they bought ice cream.

4. Whenever he runs in cold weather he gets a sore throat.

5. Because they were late they didn't get any food.

6. If it rains tomorrow we'll have to cancel the trip.

Commas are also used to introduce and to close a friendly letter. Examples: "Dear Mrs. Johnson," or "Sincerely yours," or "Yours truly,".

CHALLENGE

In the following passage, there are commas necessary for a variety of reasons as stated in the rules. Read the passage carefully and insert commas where necessary.

There are 17 commas needed.

The Wax Museum

"Is everyone ready?" asked Miss Jackson. She then announced "The bus is waiting outside." The students put on their coats picked up their knapsacks pulled out their bus tickets and formed a line. Whenever the students took a class trip they were very excited. Today they were going to visit the wax museum located in Niagara Falls Ontario. The museum was very interesting because it had numerous famous people displayed in wax form. John Lennon Elvis Presley John F. Kennedy and Pierre Elliot Trudeau were a few of the famous people on display. Because the wax figures were so lifelike it was a very spooky experience. One of the students screamed "That wax figure moved!" We all heard this and ran outside. Because we had now left the museum the teacher suggested that we eat lunch. After lunch we walked to the park looked at the Falls and returned to the bus. Although our trip was shortened by the scary incident we had a good time.

The **Semicolon** takes the place of a conjunction. It joins two independent clauses. It is best to use a semicolon with clauses that are closely related in meaning. Semicolons are also used when one independent clause completes or adds to the information of another independent clause.

Using a semicolon will help you avoid writing a run-on sentence.

Example: I enjoy playing sports; however, I have injured my knee.

Exercise D

Join the pairs of clauses to form sentences using semicolons.

Notice that each independent clause has a subject and a verb; therefore, each independent clause is a proper sentence. Choose independent clauses that are either common in subject or add more information to the first independent clause.

Column A

1. I bought her a birthday gift
2. Hockey is my favourite sport
3. She was the smartest girl in the class
4. The teacher arrived late today
5. Never before have we had such weather
6. It was a great celebration
7. The students assembled in the gymnasium
8. The buses were running late
9. My dog loves to run
10. Look up to the sky
11. The dentist gave him a needle

Column B

- her car broke down
- you can see the Milky Way
- the principal was going to speak to them
- his face went numb
- I love to stick-handle the puck
- he really likes to fetch a ball
- she always got the highest marks
- it was something she needed
- the winds howled all night long
- we all ate cake and ice cream
- instead, we took the subway

1. _____

2. _____

3. _____

4. _____

5. _____

6. _____

7. _____

8. _____

9. _____

10. _____

11. _____

13 Capitalization, Abbreviation, and Quotation Marks

Capital Letters must be used in the following cases:

1. To begin a sentence: **H**e played the piano.
2. With proper names such as people, places, cities, towns, countries: **J**ohn **S**mith, **T**oronto, **N**ew **Y**ork **Y**ankees, **P**earson **A**irport
3. For book, song, movie, and TV show titles: **R**omeo and **J**uliet, **J**ingle **B**ells, **CFTO N**ews, **T**he **W**izard of **O**z
4. For days of the week, months of the year: **T**uesday, **O**ctober 3
5. Place capitals on short forms such as **M**r., **M**iss, **M**rs., **D**r., and **S**t.
6. Place capitals on the names of holidays such as **C**hristmas, **T**hanksgiving, and **E**aster.

Exercise A

Place capital letters where necessary in each of the following sentences. Place capitals over the small case words that you are correcting.

> The number in parentheses tells you how many capital letters are needed in each sentence.

1. mr. and mrs. smith arrived in toronto on the third of november. (5)

2. he read "the hobbit" by j.r.r. tolkien. (7)

3. "harry potter" books are very popular. (2)

4. she visited her doctor, dr. johnson, whose office was on main st. (5)

5. at christmas, the children sang "jingle bells". (4)

6. we went to the skyDome to see the blue jays play against the minnesota twins. (6)

7. he watched a show entitled "animals of africa" on discovery channel. (5)

8. on monday, we have english class and on wednesday, we have french class. (5)

9. elton john recorded "goodbye england's rose" as a tribute to princess diana. (7)

10. we watched a disney film entitled "beauty and the beast". (4)

11. mr. todd dixon, our teacher, brought his dog, spot, to school. (4)

12. our computer runs on "windows me" with microsoft word. (6)

Tricky Capitalization

1. When the kinship name of a relative precedes the proper name of the relative, both names are capitalized.

    Example: **A**unt **J**oan and **U**ncle **B**ill came for dinner.

    but not – I went to my aunt's house for dinner.

2. Government offices require capitalization: **M**inistry of **L**abour, **D**epartment of **T**ransportation, **F**ederal **B**ureau of **I**nvestigation, **C**entral **I**ntelligence **A**gency.

3. Capitalize compass points when they refer to a precise location.

    Example: He went out **W**est to find a job. He was originally from the **E**ast.

    but not – He moved to the east end of town. He visited western Europe.

4. Capitalize adjective forms of proper names such as **I**talian, **G**erman, **B**ritish, **F**rench, the **S**mith family, **P**anama **C**anal, **Y**onge **S**treet.

5. Capitalize the name of a professional title when it describes a proper noun: **D**octor **S**mith, **P**rofessor **W**illiams, **S**enator **W**right, **P**resident **B**ush, **P**rime **M**inister **J**ean **C**hretien.

Exercise B

Place capital letters where necessary in each of the following sentences. Place capitals over the small case words that you are correcting.

1. He worked for the ministry of the environment.

2. doctor richards had his office in the cn tower.

3. We boarded a plane for our trip to eastern europe.

4. He lived in the east end of toronto.

5. My aunt hilda's moved out west; I will visit her next fall.

6. uncle adam worked for parks and recreation for the town of ajax.

7. My teacher was known as professor sanderson when he taught at oxford university.

8. When we were in eastern Europe, we travelled to italy and enjoyed italian food.

9. My uncle, professor jones, sent a letter to the premier of Ontario, mike harris.

10. the channel connects britain and france.

11. Which planet is bigger, venus or mars?

12. I went to metro zoo with uncle tommy yesterday.

Common Abbreviations

The following is a list of common abbreviations that you should know:

apt. – apartment	Dr. – Drive	Pres. – President
assoc. – association	etc. – et cetera	Prof. – Professor
Ave. – avenue	ft. – foot	Rd. – Road
Blvd. – boulevard	Gov. – Governor	Sgt. – Sergeant
Capt. – Captain	Jr. – Junior	Sr. – Senior / Sister
Co. – Company	Ltd. – limited	St. – Saint / Street
cont. – continued	Mt. – Mount / Mountain	supt. – superintendent
Dr. – Doctor	No. – number	vs. – versus / against

Exercise C

Test yourself with abbreviations that are common to you. Circle the proper abbreviation for each of the following words.

1. centimetres	cnt. cm. cent.	2. ounces	ozs. ounc. oz.
3. millimetres	mill. mm. Mil.	4. quarts	qt. qts. qua.
5. pounds	pou. llb. lb.	6. feet	ft. fe. fee.
7. inches	inch. inc. in.	8. miles	mls. mil. mi.
9. kilometres	ki. km. klm.	10. kilograms	ki. km. kg.
11. litres	L. lr. li.	12. millilitres	Ml. ml. Mi.
13. Sunday	Su. Snd. Sun.	14. Monday	Mo. Mdy. Mon.
15. Tuesday	Tues. Ts. Tu.	16. Wednesday	Wedn. We. Wed.
17. Thursday	Th. Thurs. Thdy	18. Friday	Fri. Frd. Fry
19. Saturday	Sat. Sa. Sdy.	20. January	Jan. Janu. Jnry.
21. February	Febr. Fbry. Feb.	22. March	Mch. Ma. Mar.
23. April	Apr. Ap. Al.	24. May	May My. Ma.
25. June	Jun. June Jn.	26. July	Jul. Jy. Ju.
27. August	Aug. Au. Aust.	28. September	Sept. Sep. Septe.
29. October	Oct. Octob. Oc.	30. November	Nov. Novem. No.
31. December	Decm. Dec. Dbr.	32. year	y. ye. yr.

Quotation Marks

1. Use quotation marks to show a direct quotation. A direct quotation is the exact words spoken by someone else. Place the quotation marks at the beginning and end of the quotation and include the final punctuation with the quotation.

   Example: John asked, "How are you feeling today?"

   Note: (1) a comma is placed after "asked" to set off the quotation
   (2) the quotation includes only the words spoken by John
   (3) the final punctuation, the question mark, is placed inside the quotation marks

   An indirect quotation sometimes referred to as a **paraphrase** does not require quotation marks because either it does not refer to the exact words or it is not set off on its own.

   Examples: Indirect quotation: John asked me how I was feeling.
   Direct quotation: John asked, "How are you feeling today?"

2. Use quotation marks around titles of poems, plays, short stories, television programmes, film titles, songs, or titles of magazine articles.

   Examples: Shakespeare wrote "Romeo and Juliet".
   I read Morley Callaghan's story "A Cap For Steve".
   "Yesterday" by the Beatles is one of the most popular songs of all time.

Exercise D

Place quotation marks where necessary and add commas to set off quotations. Add other punctuation marks where necessary.

1. She said Please help me lift the boxes.

2. What time is it he asked.

3. I read the short story A Monkey's Paw by W.W. Jacobs.

4. We found travel information in the magazine article Skiing in the Rockies.

5. The teacher stated Homework is due for tomorrow.

6. The movie The Wizard of Oz is a family favourite.

7. Where are you going for your summer holidays asked our teacher.

8. We were singing along to Happy Birthday to You at the party.

9. Don't you know the answer asked Teddy

10. Last Christmas by George Michael is a nice song.

11. Can you tell me who wrote Julius Caesar?

14 Tips for Effective Writing

 Wordiness

One simple rule of effective writing is to keep sentences simple and easy to understand. Some students use unnecessary, extra words to make a simple statement.

This writing problem is also referred to as "padded language".

Example: He was late due to the fact that the bus failed to arrive on time.

Correction: He was late because the bus was late.

Exercise A

In each of the following sentences, replace the wordy phrase with a simple word from the word bank below.

before	now	often	because
until	think	by	although

1. He will wait until such time as the train arrives.

_____

2. They travelled across Canada by means of a car.

_____

3. Prior to the time of the game, no fans had arrived.

_____

4. I am of the opinion that she should be chosen as the class representative.

_____

5. At this point in time we will leave for school.

_____

6. Due to the fact that it was his birthday, there was a big party.

_____

7. He would on many occasions walk to school alone.

_____

8. In spite of the fact that he won the race, he was still not happy.

_____

Homonym Errors

Homonyms are words that sound the same but are spelled differently.

It is easy to confuse words that sound the same when writing a sentence.

Example: She couldn't find a thing to **where** to the party.

Correction: She couldn't find a thing to **wear** to the party.

Exercise B

Find the incorrect word usages in the sentences below and replace them with the proper words.

> One of the sentences below has two incorrect word usages.

1. She was so happy that she had past all her subjects.

   _____

2. He ate the hole pie all by himself.

   _____

3. In there backyard, they planted a pair tree.

   _____

4. The man with a blue tie is my principle.

   _____

5. For her birthday, she received many presence.

   _____

6. This is the last weak of school before the holidays.

   _____

7. Who's dog is barking?

   _____

8. The game was cancelled because of bad whether.

   _____

9. Its too late to make a change in our science project.

   _____

10. They worked hard for they're spending money.

   _____

Choppy Sentences

Sometimes short sentences can be effective. However, short, choppy sentences can be tiresome for the reader, and fail to build the idea sufficiently that the writer is trying to create.

Example (1): effective short sentence – It was the best time of my life.

A sentence like the one above needs to be brief to capture the importance of a single idea.

Example (2): It was a cold night. It was also windy. I decided to stay home.

These sentences should be combined to read:

Because it was a cold and windy night, I decided to stay home.

Exercise C

Combine each group of choppy sentences into one sentence. Write the revised sentence in the space provided.

1. John has skates. They are new. They were very expensive.

   _____

2. George has a job. He works part-time. He works part-time at the variety store.

   _____

3. The rain stopped. The sun came out. We continued to play the game.

   _____

4. He was the top student. He won the award. The award was given at an assembly.

   _____

5. Barbados is an island. It is a coral island. It is in the Caribbean.

   _____

6. Toronto is a large city. The population of Toronto is nearly three million.

   _____

7. The house was brick. The house had a swimming pool. The house was large.

   _____

8. Kara is a student. She attends the high school. The high school has 1,100 students.

   _____

9. The boy is tall. The boy is thin. He is rushing out of the room. The room is dark. The room is stuffy.

   _____

Double Negatives

When a negative statement involves two negative words, a double negative occurs. There should be only one negative word for each negative statement.

Example(1): He doesn't have no money.
　　　　　　Correction: He doesn't have any money.
Example(2): Lorraine can't hardly wait for the holidays.
　　　　　　Correction: Lorraine can hardly wait for the holidays.

Exercise D

Spot the double negative in each sentence. Correct the sentence and write the corrected version in the space provided.

> The negative terms are italicized. Remember, only use one negative term for each negative statement.

1. The teacher *didn't* have *no* chalk left.

　　_____

2. Ian told Gerry that it *wasn't none* of his business.

　　_____

3. Amanda *can't* tell *nobody* about what happened.

　　_____

4. "*Don't* give me *no* more work to do," he exclaimed.

　　_____

5. She *didn't* have *no* idea what time it was.

　　_____

6. I *can't* find *nothing* in the drawer.

　　_____

7. The children *weren't* going *nowhere* after school.

　　_____

8. "*Don't* do *nothing* for the time being," he said.

　　_____

15 The Descriptive Paragraph

Spatial Order

Imagine a place that you are familiar with and think of the position of objects in that place. Now, think of descriptive words (colour, size, shape, texture, positioning) that could be used to describe these objects. When you describe the place focusing on these objects in the order that they appear, you are using spatial order as a means of composing a description.

Think of a camera panning a room. The details of that room would appear on camera in the order that they appear in the room, and the details of those objects would be visible to the camera.

Exercise A

Choose a room in your home that you would like to describe. Pretend you are a camera moving around the room. Describe, in detail, objects in the room.

Make sure that you are describing details in the order they appear. Remember to introduce your paragraph with a topic sentence that tells the reader what you are about to describe.

HINTS:

1. Use words and phrases such as over, under, beneath, on top of, beside, next to, which will give exact details about the position of your objects.

2. Try to use at least one descriptive word for each object you describe (colour, size, shape, texture).

Title: _____

Topic sentence: _____

_____ .

_____

_____

_____

_____

_____

The Narrative Paragraph

A narrative paragraph is one that basically tells a story – the relating of events that have happened. Narrative paragraphs might include detailed descriptions, but their purpose is to entertain by telling a story.

Chronological Order

Chronological order refers to the telling of events in the order in which they happen according to time. This method is most often used when writing a narrative paragraph.

If, for example, you choose to write a story about a holiday event, you might follow this order of narration:

1. describe preparations for your trip
2. tell of events during your travel
3. describe your destination upon arrival
4. tell of an event that happened while at your holiday destination
5. describe your return trip home

Compose a narrative paragraph outlining an event that happened to you. Present the details of this event in the order in which they happened according to time. Use as many descriptive details as possible to help the reader visualize the details of your story.

> It is often easier to write about an event that actually happened to you.

Title: _____

Topic sentence: _____

_____ .

_____

_____

_____

_____

_____

_____

_____

_____

_____

The Explanatory Paragraph

The purpose of an explanatory paragraph is to give a detailed explanation of the way something is done. Often in an explanatory paragraph, the method is to explain a process, step by step.

If, for example, you are explaining how to do something, then the logical thing to do is to use chronological (time sequence) order – that is, the order in which things should be done.

You may use transitional words such as: next, then, when, after, afterwards.

Exercise C

Choose a task that you can explain. Give a step-by-step, detailed explanation from start to finish of exactly how to complete the task.

Suggested Topics

Learning How to Skate	Building a Snow Fort
Loading a Computer Game	Building a Backyard Rink
Creating a Piece of Art	Baking a Cake

Title: _____

Topic sentence: _____

_____ .

_____

_____

_____

_____

_____

_____

_____

_____

_____

_____

_____

_____

_____

Letter Writing

Letters are usually classified as either **business** or **friendly**.

The friendly letter consists of the following parts:

1. A heading: the address of the person you are writing to
2. Salutation: an opening greeting (usually Dear...)
3. Body: the text of the letter
4. Closing: usually Yours truly or sincerely
5. Signature

Example Format:

1 33 Briar Hill Road, Toronto, Ontario, M4E 2L6

Date:

2 Dear Paul,

3

4 Yours truly,

5

Exercise D

Write a letter to a friend, relative, or family member telling of an event or describing something.

Dear _____ ,

Progress Test 2

Verbals

Exercise A

State the part of speech for each underlined verbal in the following sentences. Circle your answer from the three choices.

1. <u>Walking</u> is good exercise.

| noun | adjective | adverb |

2. <u>To speak</u> in public can be frightening.

| noun | adjective | adverb |

3. The horse trotted up to the <u>watering</u> hole.

| noun | adjective | adverb |

4. He discovered the <u>lost</u> treasure.

| noun | adjective | adverb |

5. She loved <u>to skate</u> on the frozen lake.

| noun | adjective | adverb |

6. Uncle Nike has repaired the <u>broken</u> vase.

| noun | adjective | adverb |

Participle Phrases

Exercise B

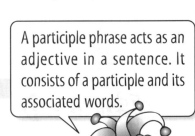

A participle phrase acts as an adjective in a sentence. It consists of a participle and its associated words.

Underline the participle phrase in each sentence below.

1. The garden was filled with flowers.
2. People waiting for the bus were getting impatient.
3. Laughing at the clown, the children were entertained.
4. The dog running across the road was nearly hit by a car.
5. The pop star waved at the waving fans.
6. The firefighters tried to get the child out of the burning house.

Exercise C

Complete each of the following sentences with a verbal of your choice.

1. _____ is good exercise.
2. He wanted _____ new hockey equipment.
3. She bought _____ paper from the stationery store.
4. The children enjoy _____ on the swings.

5. _____ with a friend is fun.

6. Their house had a large _____ area on the main floor.

7. The gifts were _____ in the cupboard.

8. The boy wanted _____ a professional athlete when he grew up.

Sentence Structure

Exercise D

Correct the run-on sentences by doing one of the following:

1. add proper punctuation
2. change the sentence into two sentences
3. change one of the independent clauses to a dependent (subordinate) clause.

Change the wording of a sentence if it corrects the run-on problem and clarifies the meaning.

1. Don't ask questions you should listen to all the information first.

   _____

2. We woke up early packed our bags jumped in the car and left.

   _____

3. The students went to the zoo they saw exotic animals it was a great day.

   _____

4. The circus came to town they had many great acts we enjoyed them.

   _____

5. Boys play basketball girls play volleyball they do these activities at recess.

   _____

Progress Test 2

Sentence Combining

Exercise E

Combine each short sentence grouping into one sentence.

> Some sentences can be converted to single word adjectives. Often a conjunction (and, or, but) is useful for combining short sentences.

1. The students were hungry. The students ate lunch. The students ate in the park.

    _____

2. The dog barked. The dog barked at the mailman. The mailman was friendly.

    _____

3. The night came. The night was cold. The wind blew.

    _____

4. Susan was a new student. She was new to our school. She came to school today.

    _____

5. Hockey is a popular sport. Hockey is popular in Canada.

    _____

Punctuation

> There are four kinds of sentences: declarative, imperative, interrogative, and exclamatory.

Exercise F

Identify the sentence type and place the proper punctuation at the end of each sentence.

1. What time is it   _____

2. Look out   _____

3. I am taking my dog for a walk   _____

4. You don't play chess, do you   _____

5. Stay where you are   _____

6. Don't you touch my drawing   _____

7. Have you ever been to Banff   _____

Contractions

Exercise G

Fill in the chart with the proper contractions.

Expanded Form	Contraction	Expanded Form	Contraction
1. will not	_____	2. did not	_____
3. has not	_____	4. we are	_____
5. she has	_____	6. we have	_____
7. cannot	_____	8. could not	_____
9. was not	_____	10. they are	_____
11. I am	_____	12. he is	_____
13. it is	_____	14. do not	_____

Colons and Semicolons

Exercise H

In each space provided, enter a colon or a semicolon.

1. The following were needed for the party __ paper plates, drinks, hot dogs, and cake.

2. The train arrived from Montreal __ it was full of French speaking passengers.

3. The hockey game went into overtime __ suddenly, John scored the winning goal.

4. The teacher had just one request __ the hard work of his students.

5. At 3 __ 30 pm the bell will ring __ we will be dismissed from school.

6. It was 12 __ 45 and we were hungry __ thankfully, lunch was finally served.

7. He witnessed the most beautiful sight __ the sunset over the ocean.

8. They were exhausted from the long walk __ a soak in a hot tub was welcome.

Progress Test 2

Possessives

Exercise I

Circle the correct possessive form of the nouns below.

1. people | peoples' people's
2. her | her's hers
3. Louis | Louis' Louis's
4. doctors | doctors' doctor's
5. player | player's players'
6. players | players' players's
7. class | class's class'
8. men | mens' men's

Comma Use

> The number in parentheses tells you the number of commas missing in each sentence.

Exercise J

Add the comma(s) needed in each sentence below.

1. On July 10 2003 they will celebrate an anniversary and go out for dinner. (2)
2. Although they were the first to arrive no one noticed them. (1)
3. Jeff asked "Is the appointment for August 2 2002 or is it for a later date?" (3)
4. The tool kit included: a wrench a hammer nails and a screwdriver. (3)
5. Unless you change the time no one will be able to attend the meeting. (1)
6. Hammerhead Peter's bulldog is very playful in spite of his fierce look. (2)

Quotation Marks

Exercise K

Place quotation marks where needed in the following sentences.

1. Sam asked, Who will be on my team?
2. We went to see Beauty and the Beast.
3. We sang Happy Birthday to You.
4. Sasha stated, I don't think I can go swimming today.
5. Our class read the short story A Day on the Farm.
6. We could have won the game, said the dejected captain.

Apostrophes

The number at the end of the sentence in parentheses indicates how many apostrophes are missing.

Exercise L

In each sentence below, add the missing apostrophe(s).

1. Hes the best player on our team but he doesnt know it. (2)

2. He borrowed Pauls book and hasnt returned it yet. (2)

3. Its about time you took your dog to get its new collar. (1)

4. When its time to go, youll know it. (2)

5. He wasnt always a student at our school; he arrived in 99. (2)

Exercise M

Re-write the following paragraph adding the missing punctuation marks.

The Grade six students were looking eagerly forward to Friday Ms Patterson their teacher promised to take them to the Science Centre However the children had to do some research first You should work in groups of three or four and each group has to find the information on this worksheet explained Ms Patterson Can we get it from the Internet asked Jenny Sure answered Ms Patterson but you must double check the information because not all the information on the Net is accurate

_____

_____

_____

_____

_____

_____

Answers

1 Nouns and Noun Use

A. 1. collective   2. proper   3. collective
   4. simple   5. compound   6. collective
   7. collective   8. simple   9. proper
   10. compound   11. simple   12. collective

B. 1. brother-in-law ; fireman
   2. classroom ; tomato plant ; window sill
   3. fire insurance
   4. bedroom ; fireplace
   5. seat belt
   6. flashlight
   7. baby-sitter
   8. grade eight ; high school
   9. motorcycle
   10. great-grandchild ; grandmother

C. 1. flock   2. army   3. navy
   4. group   5. audience   6. jury
   7. family   8. orchestra   9. crowd
   10. team   11. class   12. committee

D. 1. protects   2. visit   3. plays
   4. choose   5. applauds   6. find
   7. eat   8. go

E. 1. ships ; 1   2. knives ; 7   3. heroes ; 4
   4. countries ; 6   5. cowboys ; 5   6. bushes ; 2
   7. zoos ; 3

F. 1. singer   2. runner   3. dancer
   4. swimmer   5. hiker   6. teacher
   7. baker   8. climber   9. driver
   10. worker

Challenge
   1. artist   2. typist
   3. mathematician   4. author

2 Pronouns

A. 1. they   2. they   3. me
   4. their   5. it   6. they

B. 1. which   2. Which
   3. Where   4. this
   5. Those   6. When ; which
   7. Who; where / when   8. Where ; This

C. 1. which   2. which
   3. who   4. which
   5. who   6. which
   7. which   8. who

D. 1. ourselves   2. himself
   3. themselves   4. ourselves
   5. itself

Challenge
   1. myself -> me   2. myself -> I
   3. (Correct)   4. Delete "Myself"
   5. (Correct)   6. Himself -> He
   7. myself -> me
   No. 5

E. 1. Whose   2. my   3. I
   4. Whoever   5. me   6. us
   7. whom   8. I   9. whomever
   10. they ; we   11. yours

3 Descriptive Words and Phrases

A. 1. The <u>sly</u> fox slipped (quietly) through the woods.
   2. The <u>black</u> cloud hovered (menacingly) over the <u>playing</u> field.
   3. John, the <u>oldest</u> boy in the class, spoke (confidently).
   4. The boys (often) enjoyed playing <u>exciting</u> <u>computer</u> games.
   5. The <u>red</u> bicycle (suddenly) broke down in the middle of the trip.
   6. They (carefully) entered the <u>cold</u>, <u>dark</u> cave.
Challenge
   1. adjective   2. adverb
   3. adverb   4. adjective

B. 1. The walk <u>to the store</u> was very difficult (during the storm).
   2. (In the morning), the animals <u>in the barn</u> were fed.
   3. The leader <u>of the pack</u> was the large grey wolf.
   4. The pens <u>in the desk</u> were the property <u>of the boy</u> <u>in the third row</u>.
   5. (At the game), we ate our lunch <u>of sandwiches and cookies</u>.
   6. (During his speech), he dropped the notes <u>of the project</u>.
Challenge
   1. again   2. together   3. up
   4. back   5. up

C. 1. into   2. differed from   3. entered at
   4. stays at   5. among   6. with
   7. Besides   8. entered into   9. beside

D. (Suggested answers)
   1. annual   2. final   3. senior
   4. special   5. bright   6. sunny
   7. quickly   8. local   9. early
   10. challenging   11. silly   12. fun
   13. gladly   14. blue   15. hungry
   16. generously   17. huge   18. lucky
   19. clear   20. Suddenly   21. dark
   22. slowly   23. ferociously   24. wildly

4 Understanding Verb Forms

A. 1. makes   2. needed   3. wished
   4. play   5. arrived   6. is
   7. cost

B. 1. is   2. requires   3. is
   4. are   5. is   6. plays
   7. have   8. realize

C. 1. were   2. was   3. has
   4. is   5. has   6. are

D. 1. are ; are   2. was   3. wants
   4. want   5. agrees   6. has

E. 1. Active   2. Passive   3. Active
   4. Passive   5. Passive

F. 1. They <u>finished</u> their (homework) before going out to play.
   2. He <u>sailed</u> his (boat) across the lake.
   3. Whenever it is cold outside, she <u>wears</u> a heavy (sweater).
   4. If we don't play well, we <u>will lose</u> the (game).
   5. <u>Are</u> you <u>eating</u> your (dinner) now?
   6. He <u>ate</u> (meat) and (potatoes) for supper.

G. 1. watched – TR   2. was thrown – INT
   3. won – TR   4. watched – INT ; lost – TR
   5. arrived – INT ; unpacked – TR
   6. sang – INT ; were delighted – INT
   7. were – INT

Challenge
   1. Flowers were gathered from the garden by the children.
   2. Her friends were met by her at the bus stop.
   3. The scraps on the table were eaten by the dog.
   4. The clown entertained the children.

5   Verb Tenses

A. 1. Paula is walking to school instead of taking the bus.
   2. I have a new bicycle.
   3. She has been walking her dog in the park.
   4. We have been swimming in the lake.
   5. My friends and I are planning to have a party.
   6. My dog has been chasing the ball.
B. 1. were playing   2. shone
   3. had been arriving   4. had watched
   5. had been visiting   6. helped
   7. had done   8. were having
   9. had tried
C. 1. will wait   2. will have been played
   3. will have given   4. will go
   5. will have wanted   6. will watch out
   7. will have been congratulating
   8. will have paced
D. (Individual writing)
Challenge
   (Individual writing)

6   The Sentence and Its Parts

A. 2. The (cute) kitten | was playing (with a ball of wool).
   3. The (old) building | was being demolished (by the wrecking crew).
   4. The (uncertain) weather | caused a delay (in our plans).
   5. Water-skiing | is difficult if you are a beginner.
   6. We | walked two miles (to get to town).
   7. The (hot) sun | shines (brightly) (in the sky).
   8. I | was laughing (at the clown).
B. 1. An   2. the   3. the
   4. an   5. a   6. a
C. 1. lunch   2. (students) ; assignment
   3. (him) ; welcome   4. (children) ; treats
   5. (friend) ; truth   6. equipment
   7. (passengers) ; news   8. (us) ; ticket
   9. us
D. 1. morning ; school   2. water
   3. shore   4. class ; recess
   5. hill ; horizon ; ocean   6. night ; moonlight
E. 1. B   2. A   3. B
   4. A ; A   5. B ; B   6. B
Challenge
   1. A ; C ; B ; E ; G ; J
   2. A ; B ; D ; E ; G ; J

   3. A ; C ; B ; D ; E ; J ; F ; J
   4. A ; B ; E ; G ; J ; J ; J
   5. A ; B ; D ; E ; A ; B ; D
   6. C ; B ; D ; E ; F ; J ; I ; E
   7. B ; E ; G ; J ; F

7   Compound and Complex Sentences

A. 1. and saw a squirrel climb a tree.
   2. so we could go out and play.
   3. because we all played games.
   4. if I study very hard for the test.
B. 1. IC   2. DC   3. DC   4. DC
   5. IC   6. IC   7. IC   8. DC
   9. IC   10. DC   11. DC   12. IC
   13. DC   14. IC
C. 1. clause   2. phrase   3. sentence
   4. clause   5. sentence   6. sentence
   7. phrase   8. clause
D. 1. ADV   2. ADV   3. ADJ
   4. ADV   5. ADJ   6. ADV
E. (Individual writing)
F. (Individual writing)

Progress Test 1

A. 1. simple   2. simple   3. simple
   4. compound   5. simple   6. collective
   7. proper   8. proper   9. compound
   10. collective   11. collective   12. collective
   13. proper   14. proper
B. 1. boats   2. oxen   3. women
   4. coaches   5. bushes   6. heroes
   7. wives   8. knives   9. zoos
   10. shoes   11. cliffs   12. ladies
C. 1. baker   2. creator   3. designer
   4. player   5. thinker   6. swimmer
   7. teacher   8. helper   9. planner
   10. builder   11. speaker   12. liar
D. 1. their   2. they   3. our
   4. its   5. them   6. their
   7. me
E. 1. Which – interrogative   2. Who – interrogative
   3. those – demonstrative   4. that – relative
   5. who – relative   6. herself – reflexive
F. 1. frightened ; loudly   2. tall ; completely
   3. cheerful ; happily   4. sly ; cleverly
   5. threatening ; menacingly
G. 1. The bird in the bush sang a song of the wild.
   2. (Under the carpet), he hid his gift of money.
   3. (In the middle of the night), it began raining.
   4. The choir of St. Michael's sang (in the church) (near the village).
H. 1. between   2. into   3. from
   4. in   5. on
I. 1. wishes   2. play   3. is
   4. want   5. makes   6. chooses
   7. write
J. 1. Patricia's father drove the car.
   2. I drew that picture on the wall.
   3. The birthday cake was made by Sam's mother.

4. The tree in the backyard was planted by us.
5. The naughty children set off the alarm.

K. 1. transitive   2. intransitive   3. transitive
   4. intransitive   5. transitive   6. intransitive

L. 1. <u>dog</u> – D
   2. (her) – I ; <u>address</u> – D
   3. <u>flowers</u> – D
   4. (students) – I ; <u>homework</u> – D
   5. <u>friend</u> – D
   6. <u>me</u> – D
   7. (him) – I ; <u>bike</u> – D

M. 1. moonlight   2. table   3. rainfall
   4. movie   5. hill ; farmhouse

N. (Answers will vary.)
   1. The children stopped playing because they were too tired.
   2. I like mangoes but I don't like bananas.
   3. Jason is short but he can play basketball well.
   4. We can go there by subway or by bus.
   5. I will tell you if you don't tell anyone else.

8   Verbal, Participle, and Infinitive Phrases

A. 1. Jumping – Subj.   2. Falling – Subj.
   3. chewing – Obj.   4. Winning – Subj.
   5. sipping ; eating – Obj.   6. Singing ; dancing – Subj.
   7. making – Obj.   8. watching – Obj.
   9. Playing – Subj.

B. 1. To fly – noun   2. to speak – noun
   3. To write – noun   4. to play – adverb
   5. to come – adverb

C. 1. sleeping – giant   2. chewing – gum
   3. swaying – branches ; rustling – noises
   4. carrying – case   5. cutting – edge

D. 1. Waiting for a long time – lady
   2. climbing the stairs – man
   3. Thrilled with the outcome – winner
   4. playing in the gym – students
   5. Worried that he would be late for school – boy
   6. playing a classical tune – orchestra
   7. hoping not to get lost – He
   8. Delighted with the cake that she baked – girl
   9. Frightened by the bulldog – children
   10. carrying an umbrella – woman
   11. Hearing the bad news – actress
   12. chasing the birds – puppy
   13. Surrounded by police – robber

E. 2. Falling from a horse can be dangerous.
   3. Losing the first game upset the players.
   4. To laugh makes you feel much better when you are sad.
   5. He loves to sing in the shower.
   6. Exercising is good for both the mind and the body.

Challenge
(Individual writing)

9   Phrases – Noun, Gerund, Appositive, Absolute

A. 1. E ; Fine, colourful silk was used to make neckties.

2. F ; Hot, spicy sauce was spread on the pizza.
3. B ; She wore expensive, costume jewellery.
4. C ; Around the campfire, they told scary, ghost stories.
5. A ; Bright, colourful flags surrounded the Olympic Stadium.
6. D ; Warm, fuzzy blankets kept us warm all·night long.

B. 1. Laughing out loud – A
   2. playing the piano in front of a crowd – B
   3. keeping the news a secret – D
   4. running around the track – B
   5. Sweeping the floors – A
   6. flying a kite – C
   7. Making muffins – A

C. (Individual writing)

D. 1. The cottage we rented, <u>the one with the large front porch</u>, has a nice beach.
   2. That dog, <u>the one with the bushy tail</u>, belongs to him.
   3. He wanted a bicycle, <u>one with racing wheels</u>, for his birthday.
   4. He chose the first seat, <u>the one near the window</u>, because it had a view.
   5. His sister, <u>the one in grade three</u>, is waiting for him at the front door of the school.
   6. He drove the other car, <u>the green convertible</u>, to work every day.
   7. The players, <u>those who showed up on time</u>, got the most playing time.
   8. Snowboarding, <u>a sport for the young</u>, has become very popular.
   9. Health, <u>the thing we all desire</u>, can be achieved by eating properly.
   10. Fatigue, <u>the state of exhaustion</u>, followed her completion of the marathon.

E. (Individual writing)

F. 1. The children are fully entertained, <u>the clown having made funny balloons for everyone</u>.
   2. He ran out of the house, <u>his lunch being left behind</u>.
   3. He roared down the ice, <u>everyone trying to catch him</u>.
   4. The ice cream melted, <u>chocolate spilling everywhere</u>.
   5. The teacher handed out the report cards, <u>students waiting anxiously</u>.
   6. They lined up for the penalty shot, <u>soccer fans standing motionless</u>.
   7. <u>People running everywhere</u>, the rainstorm unleashed a heavy downpour.
   8. <u>Fans lining up for hours</u>, the tickets for the rock concert finally went on sale.

G. 1. the dog sitting up begging
   2. the runners taking their marks
   3. The contestants holding their breath
   4. Skiers dotting the hillside
   5. The end of the game coming near

10   Run-On Sentences and Sentence Combining

A. (Answers will vary.)
   1. When lunch was ready, we ate in the kitchen.
   2. The door is wide open so someone must be home.
   3. Because he has cut his foot, he put a bandage on it.
   4. When the buzzer went, the game was over.

5. She read the book about a mystery that took place in England.
6. When the train arrived at the station, it was half an hour late.
7. The weather was fine so we had a game of baseball.
8. Since it was breezy, our kites flew high in the sky.

B. (Answers will vary.)
1. The hungry cat mewed because it wanted milk.
2. The shiny, new car was red.
3. He was a grade four student of St. Patrick's School.
4. She wore a yellow ski jacket.
5. You should raise your hand to answer questions.
6. There was plenty of mathematics homework.
7. The baseball game was delayed because of rain.
8. The children participated in the 100-metre race in the schoolyard.

C. (Answers will vary.)
1. The mouse was frightened because the cat was ready to pounce.
2. The snow was like powder so the skiing was excellent.
3. The bird built a nest with twigs and bits of straw.
4. He couldn't find his key so he was locked out of the house.
5. The little girl was crying because she thought that she was lost.
6. They sailed on an ocean liner and they had a wonderful vacation.
7. They went to the baseball game and ate peanuts and cracker jacks.
8. Because the dresser drawers were full, there was not enough room for his clothes.
9. The players drank water when there was a break in the game.
10. The morning dew melted when the sun came up.

D. (Answers may vary.)
The Air Canada Centre is a large sports facility in downtown Toronto. Building of the centre started in 1997 and was finished in 1999. The Air Canada Centre is home to the Toronto Maple Leafs and the Toronto Raptors. The first hockey game played there was between the Toronto Maple Leafs and the Montreal Canadiens on February 20, 1999. The first Raptor game played in the Air Canada Centre was on February 21, 1999 against the Vancouver Grizzlies. Often there are special events, meetings, concerts, and community events going on there. The Air Canada Centre has 19,800 seats for basketball games and 18,800 seats for hockey games.

11 Punctuation (1)

A. 1. Look out! - exclamatory
2. What time is it? - interrogative
3. It was an unusually hot day. - declarative
4. What a hot day! - exclamatory
5. Never do that again. - imperative
6. Do as you are told. - imperative
7. Help! - exclamatory
8. It was nice of him to offer his help even though he was busy. - declarative
9. Do you know which team got the champion in yesterday's match? - interrogative

B. 1. couldn't   2. wouldn't   3. I would / I had
4. don't   5. can't   6. you will
7. doesn't   8. he would / he had
9. he's   10. shouldn't   11. let us
12. won't   13. isn't   14. I have
15. mustn't

C. 1. people's – 2   2. person's – 1
3. women's – 2   4. boys' – 3
5. players' – 3   6. boy's – 1
7. hers (no change)   8. class's – 4
9. Keats's – 4   10. geese's – 2
11. children's – 2   12. Dennis's – 4
13. babies' – 3   14. cat's – 1

Challenge
1. Paul's ; wasn't   2. It's ; o'clock ; isn't
3. can't ; '98   4. Susan's ; wasn't
5. she'll   6. Let's ; isn't
7. Paul's ; it's   8. I'd
9. Don't ; Louis's   10. What's

D. The day arrived for our camping trip. We packed the following items: a tent, a flashlight, a sleeping bag, and a cooler. Our guide gave us this important advice: do not leave food around the tent after dark. He also explained: "It is important to respect nature and the animals of the woodlands. Remember, you are visiting their territory. Treat it as if it was your own." We left home at 6:30 a.m. and arrived at the campsite at 11:00. It took nearly two hours to set up camp because we had to take care of the following duties: clearing the site, hammering in the tent pegs, fetching water, and setting up a campfire.

12 Punctuation (2)

A. 1. She wanted to finish school, to go to college, and to get a good job. - 2
2. We worked, ate, slept, and awoke the next day before they arrived. – 2
3. We visited our relatives in Saskatoon, Alberta. – 4
4. His birthday was August 14, 1992. – 4
5. We ate soup, sandwiches, cake, and ice cream for lunch. – 1
6. Dad, will you drive me to my friend's house? – 3
7. Playing hockey, going skiing, and snowboarding are my favourite things to do. – 1
8. The Raptors, the Leafs, and the Argos all play in Toronto, Ontario. – 1 ; 4

B. 1. "What do you want to eat for supper?" his mother asked.
2. "I wish we had school during the summer," said Susan.
3. "Don't touch that wire!" screamed the electrician.
4. "Do you have any apples, pears, or oranges?" asked the lady.
5. "Be careful!" he shouted. "There are snakes, spiders, and rats in the pit."
6. "We have to go now," Danny said.

C. 1. While he was walking home,
2. while they cheered at the hockey game
3. After they watched the movie,
4. Whenever he runs in cold weather,
5. Because they were late,
6. If it rains tomorrow,

Challenge

"Is everyone ready?" asked Miss Jackson. She then announced, "The bus is waiting outside." The students put on their coats, picked up their knapsacks, pulled out their bus tickets, and formed a line. Whenever the students took a class trip, they were very excited. Today, they were going to visit the wax museum located in Niagara Falls, Ontario. The museum was very interesting because it had numerous famous people displayed in wax form. John Lennon, Elvis Presley, John F. Kennedy, and Pierre Elliot Trudeau were a few of the famous people on display. Because the wax figures were so lifelike, it was a very spooky experience. One of the students screamed, "That wax figure moved!" We all heard this and ran outside. Because we had now left the museum, the teacher suggested that we eat lunch. After lunch, we walked to the park, looked at the Falls, and returned to the bus. Although our trip was shortened by the scary incident, we had a good time.

D. 1. I bought her a birthday gift; it was something she needed.
2. Hockey is my favourite sport; I love to stick-handle the puck.
3. She was the smartest girl in the class; she always got the highest marks.
4. The teacher arrived late today; her car broke down.
5. Never before have we had such weather; the winds howled all night long.
6. It was a great celebration; we all ate cake and ice cream.
7. The students assembled in the gymnasium; the principal was going to speak to them.
8. The buses were running late; instead, we took the subway.
9. My dog loves to run; he really likes to fetch a ball.
10. Look up to the sky; you can see the Milky Way.
11. The dentist gave him a needle; his face went numb.

13 Capitalization, Abbreviation, and Quotation Marks

A. 1. Mr. and Mrs. Smith arrived in Toronto on the third of November.
2. He read "The Hobbit" by J.R.R. Tolkien.
3. "Harry Potter" books are very popular.
4. She visited her doctor, Dr. Johnson, whose office was on Main St.
5. At Christmas, the children sang "Jingle Bells".
6. We went to the SkyDome to see the Blue Jays play against the Minnesota Twins.
7. He watched a show entitled "Animals of Africa" on Discovery Channel.
8. On Monday, we have English class and on Wednesday, we have French class.
9. Elton John recorded "Goodbye England's Rose" as a tribute to Princess Diana.
10. We watched a Disney film entitled "Beauty and the Beast".
11. Mr. Todd Dixon, our teacher, brought his dog, Spot, to school.

12. Our computer runs on "Windows ME" with Microsoft Word.

B. 1. He worked for the Ministry of the Environment.
2. Doctor Richards had his office in the CN Tower.
3. We boarded a plane for our trip to eastern Europe.
4. He lived in the east end of Toronto.
5. My aunt Hilda's moved out West; I will visit her next fall.
6. Uncle Adam worked for Parks and Recreation for the town of Ajax.
7. My teacher was known as Professor Sanderson when he taught at Oxford University.
8. When we were in eastern Europe, we travelled to Italy and enjoyed Italian food.
9. My uncle, Professor Jones, sent a letter to the Premier of Ontario, Mike Harris.
10. The Chunnel connects Britain and France.
11. Which planet is bigger, Venus or Mars?
12. I went to Metro Zoo with Uncle Tommy yesterday.

C. 1. cm.   2. oz.   3. mm.   4. qt.
5. lb.   6. ft.   7. in.   8. mi.
9. km.   10. kg.   11. L.   12. ml.
13. Sun.   14. Mon.   15. Tues.   16. Wed.
17. Thurs.   18. Fri.   19. Sat.   20. Jan.
21. Feb.   22. Mar.   23. Apr.   24. May
25. Jun.   26. Jul.   27. Aug.   28. Sept.
29. Oct.   30. Nov.   31. Dec.   32. yr.

D. 1. She said, "Please help me lift the boxes."
2. "What time is it?" he asked.
3. I read the short story "A Monkey's Paw" by W.W. Jacobs.
4. We found travel information in the magazine article "Skiing in the Rockies".
5. The teacher stated, "Homework is due for tomorrow."
6. The movie "The Wizard of Oz" is a family favourite.
7. "Where are you going for your summer holidays?" asked our teacher.
8. We were singing along to "Happy Birthday to You" at the party.
9. "Don't you know the answer?" asked Teddy.
10. "Last Christmas" by George Michael is a nice song.
11. Can you tell me who wrote "Julius Caesar"?

14 Tips for Effective Writing

A. 1. He will wait until the train arrives.
2. They travelled across Canada by car.
3. Before the game, no fans had arrived.
4. I think she should be chosen as the class representative.
5. Now we will leave for school.
6. Because it was his birthday, there was a big party.
7. He would often walk to school alone.
8. Although he won the race, he was still not happy.

B. 1. past → passed   2. hole → whole
3. there → their ; pair → pear
4. principle → principal   5. presence → presents
6. weak → week   7. Who's → Whose
8. whether → weather   9. Its → It's
10. they're → their

C. (Answers will vary.)
1. John has expensive, new skates.
2. George has a part-time job working at the variety store.

3. When the rain stopped and the sun came out, we continued to play the game.
4. He won the award for top student given at the assembly.
5. Barbados is a coral island in the Caribbean.
6. Toronto is a large city with a population of nearly three million.
7. The large, brick house had a swimming pool.
8. Kara attends a high school that has 1,100 students.
9. The tall, thin boy is rushing out of the dark, stuffy room.

D. (Answers will vary.)
1. The teacher didn't have any chalk left.
2. Ian told Gerry that it wasn't any of his business.
3. Amanda can't tell anybody about what happened.
4. "Don't give me any more work to do," he exclaimed.
5. She didn't have any idea what time it was.
6. I can't find anything in the drawer.
7. The children weren't going anywhere after school.
8. "Don't do anything for the time being," he said.

15 The Descriptive Paragraph

A. (Individual writing)
B. (Individual writing)
C. (Individual writing)
D. (Individual writing)

Progress Test 2

A. 1. noun   2. noun   3. adjective
   4. adjective   5. noun   6. adjective
B. 1. filled with flowers   2. waiting for the bus
   3. Laughing at the clown   4. running across the road
   5. waving fans   6. burning house
C. (Individual writing)
D. (Suggestions only)
   1. Don't ask questions; you should listen to all the information first.
   2. We woke up early, packed our bags, jumped in the car and left.
   3. The students went to the zoo; they saw exotic animals. It was a great day.
   4. The circus came to town. They had many great acts and we enjoyed them.
   5. At recess, boys play basketball and girls play volleyball.
E. (Suggestions only)
   1. The hungry students ate lunch in the park.
   2. The dog barked at the friendly mailman.
   3. The cold night came and the wind blew.
   4. Susan, a student new to our school, came today.
   5. Hockey is a popular sport in Canada.
F. 1. ? ; interrogative   2. ! ; exclamatory
   3. . ; declarative   4. ? ; interrogative
   5. . ; imperative   6. ! ; exclamatory
   7. ? ; interrogative
G. 1. won't   2. didn't   3. hasn't   4. we're
   5. she's   6. we've   7. can't   8. couldn't
   9. wasn't   10. they're 11. I'm   12. he's
   13. it's   14. don't
H. 1. :   2. ;   3. ;   4. :
   5. : ;   6. : ;   7. :   8. ;

I. 1. people's   2. hers   3. Louis's
   4. doctors'   5. player's   6. players'
   7. class's   8. men's
J. 1. On July 10, 2003, they will celebrate an anniversary and go out for dinner.
   2. Although they were the first to arrive, no one noticed them.
   3. Jeff asked, "Is the appointment for August 2, 2002, or is it for a later date?"
   4. The tool kit included: a wrench, a hammer, nails, and a screwdriver.
   5. Unless you change the time, no one will be able to attend the meeting.
   6. Hammerhead, Peter's bulldog, is very playful in spite of his fierce look.
K. 1. Sam asked, "Who will be on my team?"
   2. We went to see "Beauty and the Beast".
   3. We sang "Happy Birthday to You".
   4. Sasha stated, "I don't think I can go swimming today."
   5. Our class read the short story "A Day on the Farm".
   6. "We could have won the game," said the dejected captain.
L. 1. He's the best player on our team but he doesn't know it.
   2. He borrowed Paul's book and hasn't returned it yet.
   3. It's about time you took your dog to get its new collar.
   4. When it's time to go, you'll know it.
   5. He wasn't always a student at our school; he arrived in '99.
M. The Grade six students were looking eagerly forward to Friday. Ms Patterson, their teacher, promised to take them to the Science Centre. However, the children had to do some research first. "You should work in groups of three or four, and each group has to find the information on this worksheet," explained Ms Patterson. "Can we get it from the Internet?" asked Jenny. "Sure," answered Ms Patterson, "but you must double check the information because not all the information on the Net is accurate."